Joy Rainey

JOY ACROSS AMERICA
One Woman's Amazing Journey

Foreword by

Sir Stirling Moss OBE

Birlingham Books

First published in February 2014

A catalogue record for this book is available from the British Library

ISBN: 978-0-9928066-0-6

Published by Birlingham Books,
Orchard Farm, Longdon Hill, Evesham,
Worcestershire, WR11 7RP, UK
E-mail: joy@joy-across-america.com
Website: www.joy-across-america.com

Printed in Great Britain by
Quorum Print Services Ltd., Cheltenham, Glos. GL51 8PL

CONTENTS

DEDICATION

I dedicate this book to my late husband,
my dearest friend and soul-mate Trevor Hulks.

FOREWORD

by Sir Stirling Moss OBE

I first met Joy Rainey in 1959, at a race meeting at Roskilde in Denmark. She was there with her father Murray, who was racing his Cooper-Norton while I was driving my Cooper Monaco. Despite our motorsport activities taking completely different paths I was aware of her subsequent success in hillclimbing, particularly at Shelsley Walsh, where I first competed back in 1948 in my own 500cc Cooper and where she held the Ladies' record for an amazing 22 years.

I also knew of Joy's success in long distance rallies, particularly in completing the 2004 London/Sydney Marathon in a Morris Minor, so I was most impressed when I heard of her proposed trans-America trip in a 1904 Oldsmobile. Like Joy, I have taken part in the VCC's London to Brighton Run, but a 3000 mile trip in a 7 horsepower veteran car is a whole lot different to a 60 mile jaunt to the south coast!

I understand that she remains the only woman ever to cross the American continent coast to coast in a single cylinder car. Quite an achievement for one of the most remarkable and determined lady competitors I have ever known. Thank goodness she didn't turn to Formula One!

Stirling Moss

INTRODUCTION

The 2004 London to Sydney Marathon was one of the most challenging activities I have ever attempted in my life. Although I'd competed in motorsport events for a number of years it was unusual, I was told, for someone of the female gender to enter a 10,000 mile car rally as an introduction to endurance events. "Better to enter a couple of shorter rallies first, to see if you like it," was the advice.

But my advisor hadn't reckoned on my dogged determination. I wanted to drive in this particular rally and arrive at the destination, Sydney, as Australia was the country of my birth.

Over the following twelve months Trevor, my partner of over twenty years, and I set about raising sponsorship in order to buy a car, prepare it and be on the startline ready for the flag to drop. This we achieved, after many setbacks, although many of the other competitors at the start of this epic journey seemed bemused at our choice of car – a 1970 Morris Minor.

"Waste of an entry, they'll never get there" were the mutterings just before we set off.

For thirty days the Morris Minor endured every road condition imaginable from smooth tarmacadam to rough, potholed tracks barely suitable for four-wheel-drive vehicles. We climbed and descended steep mountain tracks, drove hard along straight but unmade roads, experienced manic, suicidal traffic in India and deserted, sandy desert roads in outback Australia, culminating in our arrival in Sydney on time, intact and without any damage, thirty days after leaving London.

On returning to England, strangers kept shaking our hands and congratulating us. After about a week had passed I started to think that maybe, just maybe, completing our first long-distance rally was really quite an achievement. After several more weeks I started to suffer from the beginnings of a new addiction. I wanted to participate in another long-distance rally!

In 2006 we were offered a modern four-wheel-drive Jeep, fitted with modern luxuries such as air-conditioning and power steering, to take part in the Carrera Sudamericana. I'd never been to South America before and this rally would cross Argentina, Bolivia, Peru and Ecuador in twenty-two days. I couldn't resist the challenge. To witness the rugged scenery of the Andes and remote villages where the inhabitants dressed in vivid, coloured clothing would be a once in a lifetime experience. Yet on reflection, after the event, it seemed similar to watching a film while seated in a climate controlled box and watching the scenery as we sped through, because there was no time to stop. The locals waved as we whizzed through their villages high in the Andes but we couldn't stop and interact with them, let alone learn about their customs. And driving a modern 4x4 lacked the excitement of an unlikely vehicle like a Morris Minor without modern technical aids.

What event could we aim for next? Obviously, one that could satisfy my needs and my new addiction! Yet none of the forthcoming organised events I'd read about appealed to me.

Ever since I'd met Trevor, all those years back, he'd regularly expressed a desire to holiday in the States. However work commitments, plus other interests and responsibilities, meant that the big Apple and beyond had been off the 'places to visit' list.

Then we happened to see a newspaper advertisement promoting USA holidays. "We must," said Trevor, not for the first time, "go to the States sometime."

He looked at me with astonishment when he heard my reply.

"How about driving from San Francisco to New York in the 1904 Oldsmobile?"

I'd recently been reading a book about the first attempts to make this particular trip. Up until early 1903, no one had successfully crossed the USA in a motor vehicle; several attempts had ended in failure. The first to achieve the feat would create a great deal of publicity and possibly some financial reward. It would be a story of daring people, piloting horseless carriages of questionable reliability over unmapped tracks, sand dunes, mountains and deserts.

The first to successfully cross the vast continent was George A Wyman on a 1.5 horsepower California Motor Cycle, which was a bicycle with a small auxiliary gasoline motor, but more interest was focused on four wheel vehicles. On 27th May, a 20hp Winton set out from San Francisco. It was followed 27 days later by a 12hp Packard and finally, on 6th July, by a 4.5 hp Oldsmobile. All arrived in New York in the order they started, but the Oldsmobile encountered floods lasting for days on end which turned the tracks into thick, glutinous mud. The drivers, Lester Whitman and Eugene Hammond, reached New York in 74 days and continued on to Boston to enable Oldsmobile to claim a notable first: the first motorized vehicle to successfully drive from San Francisco to Boston.

This was a great achievement in those days considering that the roads were tracks mainly used by wagons, most of them bringing new immigrants moving west to start new lives.

In the twenty-first century, most of the route that Whitman and Hammond used in 1903 from San Francisco to New York is tarmac, but to drive a hundred and five year old motor vehicle nearly four thousand miles would still present major challenges. Unlike a modern vehicle, in which the driver and passengers are encased and protected in a steel box, a 105-year-old car is built high like a horse carriage which the driver and passengers sit on, rather than in, without any protection from the elements. And with a top speed of just 25 mph on the flat and mere crawling speed up hills or mountains, not only do the driver and passenger feel part of the scenery but they can hear the birds singing and smell the flowers and plants as they chug merrily along.

"Sounds like a good idea," was Trevor's response to my suggestion. It was the one I was expecting.

I decided to mull over the idea for about a month before making the final decision or telling anyone else. If we were to embark on such an epic journey I wanted to be certain that it could actually be achieved – or that I hadn't changed my mind in the meantime.

A month later my resolve was just as strong. I started to believe that this could be our most challenging adventure yet.

CHAPTER 1

A PLAN IS HATCHED

The decision was made. In July 2009 I would pilot our 1904 Oldsmobile Curved Dash Runabout from San Francisco to New York with Trevor as my co-driver. It would be the same team that contested our two previous endurance rallies except that this would be different; a re-enactment of the Whitman and Hammond crossing one hundred and six years earlier.

Making the decision was the easy part. But what would be the next stage? I was used to entering organised events with each night's hotel stop pre-arranged. A road book for every competitor detailed the complete route with every turn and traffic light junction listed as well as road conditions and distances to each control point. It was the co-driver's role to follow the instructions, calculate the average speed and convey the relevant information to the driver so that if nothing went wrong, we would arrive at the last control point of the day at the scheduled time.

This would be different. I quickly realised that a good deal of research would be needed. We were unable to travel to the States beforehand to carry out a route survey in a modern car, so to attempt the USA crossing for the first time in a century-old car was going to be a steep learning curve.

There was also the cost to consider; freight for the Oldsmobile, air fares, accommodation, hire of a back-up vehicle to carry spares and petrol - the list was getting bigger and the total soon reached a figure outside my financial capabilities. And what about the Oldsmobile? Before embarking on an epic journey of almost 4000 miles it would most definitely need to be rebuilt and specially prepared.

That exercise alone would be not only time-consuming but incur considerable costs.

During 1903, Oldsmobile manufactured 3750 vehicles so, at the time, spare parts were readily available. Any spares required by Whitman and Hammond had been ordered by telegram, were immediately dispatched from the factory by railway and arrived surprisingly quickly.

Spare parts for 105-year-old Oldsmobiles are, needless to say, not available in the twenty-first century. So before embarking on an adventure like this any spares, including those we would need to take with us, would need to be individually made.

The challenges were beginning to feel insurmountable and I began to think it was time to forget about this project altogether. Perhaps I wasn't feeling my normal, fairly optimistic, self on that particular day as this was completely out of character. Usually, once I've made a decision about a project, I set out to find ways of making everything achievable, yet I was now thinking of abandoning this one before it even got to the starting blocks.

Fortunately, this negative attitude disappeared before I had gone off the idea altogether and I knew my biggest challenge was about to begin – to find sponsorship. That might be more achievable than winning the Lottery!

I was shy in my youth and although maturing years have given me a little more confidence, I still find it embarrassing to ask top executives to part with company funds to enable me to go off and achieve some long held ambition.

During a phone conversation a successful businessman friend asked me, in an exasperated tone, why this was.

"It's not as if you're asking for something for nothing. They're going to get plenty of media coverage, aren't they?"

"Of course. I always work hard for my sponsors, as you know."

"Well then, get on with it. And make sure you appear confident."

He hung up, leaving me with a deep feeling of inadequacy.

On reflection I realised he was right. I really wanted to drive my 1904 Oldsmobile across the States. Agonising about details wouldn't advance the project.

I was ready to leap into unknown territory.

From the book written about the 1903 crossing I gleaned enough information to be able to plot the route. Plotting this exactly on a large scale map I was amazed at the diverse conditions we would encounter, from 8,500 ft mountains to hot, dry deserts and tracks out in the wilds, running north of the Great Salt Lake and all still in a similar condition to how they were in 1903. The more I plotted, the more my enthusiasm increased. Nothing was going to stop me now. We would be driving the Oldsmobile from San Francisco through thirteen states, including Ontario, Canada, passing over the bridge at Niagara Falls then New York State before we finally reached New York City, a total of approximately four thousand miles.

—

CHAPTER 2

EARLY DAYS WITH THE OLDS

I'd purchased my veteran Oldsmobile back in 2006.

Ever since I saw the film 'Genevieve' as a child, my fascination for the annual London to Brighton Veteran Car Run has never ceased. The event was first held in 1896 to celebrate the Parliament's passing of The Light Locomotives Act allowing motor-cars to be run on English roads at speeds not exceeding 12 mph. Over 500 pre-1905 vehicles every year from all over the world enter the event and I wanted to be in one of them.

In 2001 I couldn't believe my luck when I was offered a drive in the Haynes Motor Museum 1900 Clement. I fantasised for weeks before the event, imagining myself reaching the finish at Madeira Drive on Brighton sea-front. There would be loud applause after enduring an adventurous drive through heavy London traffic and along scenic country roads, waving to the crowds as the little De Dion powered Clement chugged majestically along. In the event, to my utter dismay the dream ended as we came to an abrupt stop half way up Streatham Hill, not many miles from the start, with a split crankcase.

I tried not to give up hope that I would have another opportunity, but after five years my optimism started to waver.

Then a conversation with someone I'd known for many years, vintage car enthusiast Michael Hallowes, revealed that he'd recently imported a 1904 Oldsmobile Curved Dash Runabout from the USA. He wasn't quite sure whether a veteran would be suitable for his stable, as he really preferred later cars producing a bit more oomph than a vehicle with just 7 horsepower. The deciding factor was the test he applies to any car he purchases – whether or not it would get to the pub up the hill from his Cotswold village house. The Oldsmobile had failed before its capability of mounting the rise was established when, with a loud clonking noise, the differential gears stripped their teeth and the car came to a sudden stop just yards from his house. The problem hadn't been resolved and I could sense that Michael had lost interest.

An invitation to a pub lunch and a viewing of the veteran resulted in my being somewhat attracted to the car. But knowing that Michael was a successful wheeler-dealer I tried to conceal my enthusiasm, as I thought the price might escalate.

"Why don't you take the back axle home with you," suggested Michael. "Trevor could start fixing it and you could have the car running for the Brighton Run."

"I haven't decided to buy the car yet." I said. "What if I decide not to and then what happens to the back axle?"

"Of course you'll buy it.".

I cast a glance at Trevor and could tell that he was enthusiastic about the possibility of acquiring a veteran.

Michael had decided that his new acquisition would be better in our hands so I didn't need much persuading when I learned that the price was right – he also had a confirmed entry in the London to Brighton Run. Although that was just one month away, I was hopeful of participating and even more hopeful of arriving at the destination.

We went home with the back axle bits and Trevor didn't object, even after having been given the task of rebuilding the back axle in a very short time. Ten days later the axle was reunited with the rest of the vehicle which was brought home complete, ready to preen for the London to

Brighton Run and to make and fit the special adaptations to enable me to drive it.

But as often happens with mechanical items, things very rarely go to plan.

I'm not sure quite what I was expecting from this 102-year-old antique. I'd heard the foot-tapping 1905 popular song 'In My Merry Oldsmobile' and I'd envisaged the single-cylinder Olds would roll happily along the road with its slow revving engine beating in time with the rhythm of the song. But I was disappointed. This Olds ran rough and unevenly, would not pick up speed, would not stay in the higher of its two gears and its brakes were virtually non-existent. Like its new owner, merry was not exactly what it was feeling.

Unlike modern sophisticated vehicles, the mechanical simplicity of early horseless carriages can enable problems to be easily detected. My trusty co-driver Trevor discovered that the carburettor float was full of fuel, the ignition timing was inconsistent, the transmission linings were made of a variety of materials, none of which were providing the necessary drive, and the brakes were lined with thin brass sheet and hence decidedly ineffective.

After much effort and man-hours over several days the correct transmission linings were fitted, carburettor float repaired, brake linings changed, ignition timing reset and the Olds seemed transformed.

After all that time-consuming mechanical activity and just days from the start of the London to Brighton Run, there had been no time for my adaptations to be finished and even that exercise was proving more complicated than expected. I wanted some practice beforehand to familiarise myself with the tiller steering and the high seating position, as well as any individual quirks the Olds may be hiding.

Three days before the Brighton Run and after plenty of

midnight oil burning, the Oldsmobile was finished and ready for the first test drive.

Situated under the seat, the engine is started by turning the starting handle mounted on the outside of the bodywork. It takes a considerable amount of effort but soon the Oldsmobile coughed, spluttered and sprung into life. Sitting up so high and without a bonnet to look over, the sensation of speed appeared much greater than I expected. I kept watching the wheels bumping up and down, the tarmac appearing to loom towards me at great speed as we chugged around the country lanes. It felt quite frightening for the first couple of miles. I couldn't get on with the tiller steering at first, having to change my body position dramatically to turn both left and right corners. I reckoned I needed a few more inches of length on my arms to drive properly. Suddenly I started to regret buying a car without a normal steering wheel.

Back home, I came to the conclusion that I wasn't capable of driving the Olds in the Brighton Run. I felt devastated.

"You can drive on Sunday, Trevor," I lamented. "I'll be your navigator.".

"Don't be daft, 'he retorted. "You know that's what you've always wanted."

"No really. It's OK. For the first time in my life I think a mechanical device is going to defeat me."

Next day, after a longer drive, I started to adapt to the car and decided that at least I would start the Brighton Run. If it wasn't going well then Trevor could take over the driving.

So on a glorious sunny day, the Oldsmobile chugged from London to Brighton without missing a beat and with me at the helm. By the end of the sixty mile event I was impressed by its mechanical agility as it negotiated its way through dense traffic and over the rolling Sussex hills, overtaking many of the other veterans on the way.

Best of all, my hang-up about driving with the tiller steering had more or less vanished although I found the steering fairly heavy and the car to want to follow the camber of the road. By the time we had arrived in Brighton my left arm felt as though it had been arm wrestling all day but at least, after many years of longing, I experienced the utter joy of reaching the Brighton finish line.

.Although my Curved Dash Oldsmobile had undergone some restoration in the States, when a new car is acquired, in this case a 102 year old vehicle, you can never be confident that all the components have been thoroughly checked. As Trevor was busy restoring his other projects, it was well into the following summer and only months before the next London to Brighton Veteran Car Run, before the Olds was brought out again.

An attendance at an Oldsmobile technical seminar given by Gary Hoonsbeen, a world renowned Curved Dash expert who had come over from the States, provided the necessary incentive to get on with the job.

Expecting routine kingpin and wheel-bearing replacement, we were dismayed to find that both the steering tiller and its attached shaft had cracked. The stub axles were also bent and showed signs of previous attempts at straightening. As with most antique vehicles, spare parts need to be manufactured and this kept Trevor busy machining bits from solid bar as well as preparing a pattern to have new stub axles cast. Two weeks before the Brighton Run the stub axles arrived from the foundry but turned out to be faulty. One week before the Brighton Run we were still waiting for the replacements, which then had to be machined.

When, a few years back, I'd retired from competitive speed hill-climbing to take up a more sedate and relaxing type of motoring, I was looking forward to giving up the high anxiety that a driver encounters when a mechanical problem occurs at the most inappropriate moment. The driver is keen to get to the start line but the mechanics are attempting to sort out the problem, time is running out and your mind is full of negative thoughts that you are not going to make it.

A few days before the Run the stub axles were delivered and Trevor managed the machining with enough time in hand for a few test runs and some minor adjustments. We set out, confident that this Oldsmobile would make it to Brighton for the second time in its life, but there were always nagging doubts in the back of my mind. This time they were compounded by the number of participating cars we passed in London parked at the side of the road in the early stages of the Run, their drivers either busy with spanners or looking totally dejected.

It was a year since I had been in my Olds and this time I'd elected to be passenger, so that Trevor could drive the complete route. But I couldn't help being impressed by the way the car loped up hills in top gear, overtaking many of the other marques. However if it got caught behind a slower vehicle and lost speed, making it necessary to change down to the lower of its two gears, it crawled up the hill and it was then difficult to regain the momentum.

Along the route, every pub in the Sussex villages seemed to be overflowing onto the pavements with partying crowds, pint in one hand and waving to us with the other. Residents were well set up in their front gardens, enjoying the unseasonable warm weather with picnic tables full of food and bottles, some offering refreshments as the horseless carriages passed by.

We managed to get to the Madeira Drive finish just before 2.00pm, after a couple of stops for fuel and with brake and carburettor adjustments along the way. What a relief to see the sea and Brighton Pier and the finish line!

All of the Oldsmobile finishers were greeted by Debbie Stephens, great granddaughter of Oldsmobile founder R E Olds, who presented us with a souvenir booklet about her great grandfather and his innovations.

But rather than use the car for just one sixty-mile event a year, I wanted to experience something a little longer. I couldn't put the idea of driving from San Francisco to New York out of my mind.

CHAPTER 3
THE REBUILD

After mulling over our proposed trip during the 2007 Christmas break, it soon became obvious that we were both really keen to start on our next adventure. The plan would be to drive the 1904 Oldsmobile from coast to coast, across the USA, during July and August 2009. That timescale would allow more than a year for planning the trip, finding sponsorship and, just as important, rebuilding and preparing the Oldsmobile for the journey of its lifetime.

An invitation to exhibit the car at Race Retro, an annual exhibition of historic racing cars and automobilia, at the end of February 2008 meant that the rebuild would have to be put on hold until after the event. I had convinced myself that it could be important to have both the Olds and ourselves on show with the possibility of meeting a potential sponsor. A number of people seemed interested in our challenge, but most were surprised that anyone could consider taking a hundred-year-old horseless carriage on such a long journey and were somewhat sceptical. Perhaps they thought we were mad, and they were probably right, but at the end of the three-day show not one mega-rich company director had shown interest in signing up for a sole sponsorship deal.

We did renew acquaintances with David Winstanley of Acceleration TV, whom we met back in 2004 when he was filming the London to Sydney Marathon and again in 2006 for the Carrera Sudamericana. David did at least say that if we were to drive such a uniquely old vehicle across the USA he would like to come and film our progress.

So it was back to the drawing board! Perhaps, I thought, I should start trying to sell sponsorship space by building a box over the rear engine cover, just like Whitman and Hammond's car in 1903, dividing it into sections and selling space in £5,000 blocks on each side and on the back. I'd calculated that we needed to raise in the region of £25,000 to cover all the costs of the trip, so all I had to do was sell five spaces on the box. Easy – or so I thought!

While I tried to come up with other clever sponsorship ideas and plan the route, Trevor got on with dismantling the Olds.

"It's quite easy to lift the body off the chassis", Gary Hoonsbeen had told us at that seminar in Lincolnshire. "Just undo four bolts, take off the tiller and a few other components and it can be lifted off".

With the aid of an overhead hoist in the workshop, Trevor had done just that only to reveal a somewhat oily mess. Nevertheless, he set to and began to dismantle this ancient piece of machinery.

One of the weakest engine components, particularly on the earlier 4.5 hp Oldsmobile, is the crankshaft. Although our 1904 model was, by comparison, a massive 7 hp and the crankshaft was sturdier, we elected to have a new one made, just to be sure it would last the journey.

Trevor contacted all the comparatively small number of crankshaft manufacturers that traded in the UK and settled for one in the Midlands. Although the prices seemed to vary somewhat, at least the particular company he'd chosen had, we understood, a good reputation.

The Olds flywheel is massive and although Trevor owned just about every known piece of workshop equipment, his press wasn't big enough to separate the flywheel from the crankshaft. The crankshaft company informed him that they had a big press. "Just deliver the crankshaft and flywheel," they said, "and we'll remove it as part of the job."

It was April before the assembly was delivered to them, together with Trevor's detailed, dimensioned crankshaft drawing. The lead time, we were told, would be nine weeks. Give or take a couple of weeks, that meant we could take delivery of the new crankshaft by the beginning of July, which would be ideal. Trevor's engineering work was always to an extremely high standard and the more of the Olds he took apart, the more he was amazed at the poor standard of the previous rebuild done in the US. He suspected it was probably assembled just to sell on and not necessarily to last. In other words, he was appalled! Similarly, the bodywork looked as if it had just been given a thin spray of paint and certainly didn't bear close inspection. The paintwork became my responsibility, so I set about rubbing down the wooden bodywork and steel mudguards right down to the base material. It sure was hard work! It took me ages and my arms felt as if they were about to fall off.

The plan was to brush-paint with coach enamel, more or less the way it had been done over a century earlier. This wasn't a new experience for me as I'd painted my modern single-seater racing car using this method, but that was more than twenty years ago and I really wanted the Oldsmobile's paintwork to end up looking as if it had been professionally done. I knew the mechanics of the vehicle would be to a high standard once Trevor had finished. The bodywork needed to match them and I became quite nervous about my ability.

I used Teckloid coach enamel. It's amazing how, when this paint is applied using the right technique with a pure bristle brush, and with the surface properly prepared, the finished product ends up smooth, shiny and with no brush marks. I have to confess, though, that my first attempt on the Olds was disappointing. I felt like a failure.

The first thing that anyone notices about a collector's car is the bodywork – they don't initially seem to notice the brilliance of the mechanical rebuild. I knew I had to get it right!

As this is not a practical guide to coach painting, I won't go into all the 'do's and don'ts'. My problem, though, seemed to emanate from the first few coats of primer filler and undercoat. Yes, I'd followed all the instructions, of which the most important was washing down the prepared surface with special cleaning thinners to remove any previously applied silicone polish. This I did religiously, at every stage, but there was always a reaction after I'd applied the final coat, leaving tiny 'blowholes'. After several weeks of rubbing back and going through the whole process again the final product was OK – not perfect, but I decided to settle for it.

One of the main hazards when brush painting is dust. I've lost count of how many times I thoroughly washed my pure bristle brush. I made Trevor leave the workshop so that no dust could be raised from the floor. I even covered myself in plastic, but I wasn't prepared to go to the extremes I went to when painting my racing car. Back then, I took each fibreglass panel into a room in the house. I'd already covered the floor with plastic, so I then completely disrobed so that no dust could come out of my clothes, covered my hair with a shower cap and got on with the painting. I did have a slight accident when the carpet and part of my naked body got covered with blue paint, but at least it was summer, so I didn't get cold. However I wasn't prepared to remove my clothes in freezing weather to use the same technique with the Oldsmobile and anyway, all this work was taking place in the workshop, not the house. Imagine if someone had called in to see how everything was going only to find a lady, naked apart from a shower cap, applying paint with a brush to a vehicle more than a century old. Initial disbelief would have been followed by a not unreasonable suspicion of madness...

Trevor was getting on well with the mechanical side and after the whole chassis was dismantled and all components cleaned and laid out on the floor, it was easier to plan what was needed.

The new valves that had been ordered arrived on time, as did several new spring leaves, but the crankshaft didn't, the completion date having been put back by another month or so. Just in case they got mislaid, Trevor decided to pick up the old crankshaft and the flywheel. He was horrified to find that instead of the old crankshaft having been carefully separated from the flywheel in a press, it had been attacked with a hammer. Our spare crankshaft was ruined. Then, on examination of the massive flywheel, Trevor noticed cracks which proper crack-testing revealed were major faults. That meant that yet another important component had to be cast and then machined – more expense and more time. Trevor drew up the flywheel, located a foundry and arranged for it to be cast, which would take another couple of months.

Then in October 2008, an opportunity arose to participate in the Karma Enduro, a charity event in India where the seventy participants got to drive brand new Hindustan Ambassadors over a 1,500 mile route starting in Goa and finishing in Cochin. When I first heard about the event I was extremely keen to participate. We'd travelled through parts of India during the London to Sydney Marathon and, surprisingly, it had emerged as my favourite country. So any opportunity to visit India again could not be refused. However with so much planning needed for our forthcoming American trip, I started to regret accepting the invitation to do the event.

With the single-cylinder Oldsmobile engine still in bits and awaiting the new crankshaft, which was needed before the white-metalling of the big-end bearing could be done, things were starting to feel stressful with all the unknowns. White-metalling is a highly skilled process involving firstly the removal of fatigued white-metal from the parent bearing, which is then tinned to ensure an effective bond. New, molten white-metal (babbit) is then gravity cast onto the bearing surface before the assembled connecting rod, complete with hinged big-end cap, is machined to fit the crankshaft journal. This last operation meant that Trevor was unable to book in our job with the Coventry Boring and Metalling company until the crankshaft had been finished.

We were eventually notified that the crankshaft was ready on the day before we were due to fly out to India. Fortunately our flight was in the evening and seven months after the crankshaft was meant to be finished, we picked it up on the way to the airport and delivered it to Coventry for the final stage of the operation. We were promised that the bearing assembly would be finished by the time we arrived back from India, and it was. At last someone had kept their word.

Once the rebuild was finished, the Oldsmobile would need considerable running on the road to iron out the inevitable problems. The testing showed that there was still a lot of work to be done. It was becoming obvious that time was running out, so we decided that there was no alternative but to postpone our USA trip until the following year, 2010.

I felt devastated as I wanted to get on with it and not wait another year, but we had to accept the situation. Weather-wise, there was only a small window in which to plan the trip. To avoid both the winter and Mid America's August tornado season, it would have to take place during July and August. At least the extra time would allow me to find more sponsorship as I was not having much success with this part of the exercise, due in part to my continued difficulty in promoting myself and my adventures.

CHAPTER 4

TRAGEDY

India was no less enjoyable the second time around. I always find the people so welcoming and willing to share with foreigners anything they might have, be it food or possessions, regardless of their financial situation.

Trevor drove the Hindustan Ambassador (a car, not a person!) and for a change, I was navigator. It certainly was a strange experience to drive a brand new car that was effectively designed in the 1950s and hadn't really progressed in the light of modern technology. The Ambassador is based on the 1956 Morris Oxford. When production stopped in the UK, all the tooling was shipped out to India and the Oxford became the Ambassador, the only car manufactured in India at the time.

All of the 70 cars supplied to our group were painted white, which meant that after we finished our rally they would be used by India's civil servants, who only drive white cars. Taxis were painted black and yellow so it was easy to identify who was who by the colour of their car.

At times during the rally, Trevor felt unwell with cramps in his abdomen and on many evenings found it necessary to go to bed quite early. The symptoms had started in the UK, where his GP had told him to take painkillers and assured him they would go away. Trevor consulted the doctor following the rally who could find no obvious problem, but by the end of the event he felt no better.

Back in the UK, Trevor's GP didn't feel unduly worried about his continuing symptoms but decided that at some stage he would arrange an appointment with a specialist. Christmas was approaching and the appointment was made for the end of January. Much too long to wait ...

During the Christmas break, with the flywheel finished Trevor got on with assembling the engine of the Oldsmobile. The chassis was looking pristine with new paintwork, complete with Trevor's professional gold lining. Waiting to be reunited with engine and bodywork, the Olds looked just as it must have done before it first left the factory back in 1904.

We talked often about our forthcoming trip and I got on with planning the route. I started to feel a trifle concerned about part of it as it seemed that for a number of days there would be no alternative to using the interstate highways. I had looked in fine detail to find alternative minor roads but there were none. It would be dangerous, not to mention illegal, to take a car with a 25 mph maximum speed along such busy roads. Imagine how frightening it would be with big trucks thundering past up to three times faster.

An invitation to visit Oldsmar, Florida prompted a change in my route planning. Oldsmar is just to the west of Tampa, Florida, and the city was founded by Ransom E Olds, the founder of Oldsmobile Engine Company, who had bought 40,000 acres of land back in 1913. It was nice to be invited for a ceremonial finish by Officials of the City of Oldsmar, but it was 1,500 miles from our intended finish in New York and it would be necessary to have the car transported there. It would, however, be an appropriate place to finish the trip and after further communication with officials, I became extremely enthusiastic about the detour.

David Winstanley, who was to film our trip, said "The route you take isn't important as all you're really focusing on is driving coast to coast. You could easily choose a more southern route." It emerged that he'd always wanted to visit Monument Valley while my lifetime ambition was to visit New Orleans. So I set about devising a new route from San Francisco, via Monument Valley and New Orleans, to arrive at

Daytona Beach to complete the Pacific/Atlantic coast-to-coast trip, then it would be on to Oldsmar for the ceremonial finish. Using Google maps, the route I finally chose offered a variety of terrain from mountains 8,500 feet above sea-level to deserts, high plateaux, tropical rain forests and flat coastal roads. I was starting to get excited about the trip but we still had more than a year to wait and I was no nearer to securing sponsorship. I was convinced that the extra time would finally bring positive results.

Trevor's health, however, was becoming a concern. The Oldsmobile rebuild was a spare-time job for him; he was more at home in the workshop every evening than he was watching television in the sitting room, but after a day's work he was becoming increasingly tired and found it difficult to continue working on hobbies. The consultation with the specialist was unsatisfactory; he was given yet more pills and told to go back to the GP to make an appointment with a different type of specialist. There was no help from the GP, so we made a decision to change to another one at a different surgery.

About this time I had to call an ambulance in the middle of the night and Trevor was taken to A&E. After two days in hospital he was sent home, but was still very ill for much of the time. Nevertheless he forced himself to work on the Oldsmobile and in April it was ready for its first road test. After a few minor adjustments, Trevor was convinced the Olds was running much smoother than before and it appeared to be producing a bit more power.

There was still quite a bit of work to be done, mainly cosmetic, and the wooden spoked wheels needed to be taken apart, checked and re-glued, but at least the majority of the mechanical re-build was finished. I took the car for my first drive on the road and it seemed a much pleasanter vehicle to drive than when it was first acquired. We were both energised and looking forward to the USA trip.

Then tragedy struck. Trevor was taken again to A&E and transferred to a ward. The men's ward was over crowded and humiliating and yet still no consultant could tell him what his health problem was. Most of the summer was spent in and out of hospital. The news slowly emerged that Trevor had cancer. It had spread to most of his organs, each one giving him such painful symptoms in different parts of his body, which then had to be operated on. In August, the decision was made that chemotherapy would start when Trevor had recovered from his latest operation. It was September 14th, his birthday, before he received his first treatment. Hardly, I suggested, the best birthday he could have had. But he whispered to me that on the contrary it was, because at last something was being done about his cancer. We agreed that on his next birthday we would have a real celebration. It was never to be. Trevor succumbed to the disease on October 27th.

I had spent every day of the previous six months visiting Trevor in hospital. I loathed seeing him suffer in the crowded wards, but he never once complained or gave up hope; I wanted to pick him up and bring him home and in my mind I was certain a miracle would happen. Sometimes, when I drove the 20 mile trip home every evening, I was full of optimism but mostly I was in deep despair. Then, on October 27th, I lost my soul-mate. He had come home a few days earlier and I sat with him 24 hours a day until the end.

My world was devastated.

CHAPTER 5

TIME TO REGROUP

I wanted to run away. I felt desperate to escape to Australia to stay with childhood friends after Trevor's funeral, but there was a problem. A week before Trevor died my mother had fallen and broken her hip. She doesn't like hospitals and convinced both herself and the medical team that she would be better off at home, which was a 'granny flat' next to my house.

The day after Trevor passed away she arrived home, although I'd tried to persuade both her and the medical team that she needed to go to a rehabilitation centre for about ten days. She refused and the medical team were also convinced that she would manage well with the carers that were already in place. I wasn't so convinced. I was also thinking of my own mental state after the traumatic year that I'd been through and I wasn't ready to look after someone else so soon. I needed space for quiet reflection and to come to terms with my life.

When my mother arrived there was no care team arranged. And she can be such a difficult patient – wanting to be independent when she can't be. She didn't take too kindly to my assistance, which of course she couldn't do without. Within days I had arranged some help, but it was still necessary for me to be there.

I'd escape sometimes to the workshop but the eerie silence, the machinery not running and Trevor not there, made me quickly return to the house. I kept expecting Trevor to appear, but he didn't. I wanted to see him, I wanted to talk to him, but I knew I would have to get used to the situation.

Each time I went into the workshop and saw the Oldsmobile I became more upset. Trevor's dream to visit the

USA could now never happen but sometimes I almost believed he would appear and ask, "Are you ready?"

I stopped going into the workshop unless I really needed to.

My desire to seek refuge somewhere else became strong – a change of scenery, different people, that's what I needed.

In February 2010 I travelled to Geelong, my hometown in Australia, to stay with my childhood friend, Joan. My mother was now mobile and could manage most things for herself and although I felt selfish about leaving, I knew that I needed this two-week escape.

It was good to reminisce about childhood and teenage years with Joan. I've never been able to understand why she didn't end up as a car nut like me. She travelled with us nearly every weekend when Dad was racing all those years ago. We had difficulty controlling our laughter when we recalled the day we pushed my father's Cooper Mk 4 up the street where we lived.

Dad had just bought a Cooper Mk 9 from the factory in Surbiton in England. While awaiting its arrival he also bought a Manx Norton engine which he'd rebuilt so it was ready when the Cooper arrived. The Mk 4 was parked on the veranda of our house, without an engine, when Joan arrived. She (or was it me?) suggested we push the Cooper up the street, coast down the hill, then turn in through the gates of our drive, which had two massive brick pillars. We would take turns to see who could get furthest up the drive towards the house. That meant the winner would be the one who used the brakes less – or not at all! We couldn't remember who won but we sure had a lot of laughs.

This two-week break to visit my hometown, meeting old friends, lunching and dining, was probably the catalyst I needed to try and find a life on my own.

About this time I had an email from Gary Hoonsbeen, the American founder of the Curved Dash Oldsmobile Club, suggesting that I might consider doing the USA trip myself as a tribute to Trevor. "I never say never," was my polite reply, but I really believed that I wouldn't attempt the trip myself, and for a number of reasons.

Firstly, I couldn't envisage doing the trip without Trevor.

Secondly, the Oldsmobile was not a 'Joy friendly' car. I was unable to start it myself or even get in (or on) it without assistance.

Thirdly, I would need a team of people to accompany me and I didn't, I thought, know anyone that would fill the bill.

Fourthly, the Olds was not quite finished or run-in and I didn't know anyone who had experience with veteran cars.

Fifthly, I would need sponsorship.

All those things convinced me that I could not, and would not, now attempt this epic journey of nearly 3000 miles across the USA.

It's strange, but the idea of finding a way to do the trip kept coming back to me from time to time. I would then question myself about whether I really wanted to do it. My reply was always in the negative.

CHAPTER 6

A PLAN IS RE-FORMED

Over the summer months I found myself going to hillclimbs at Prescott and Shelsley Walsh. I'd competed for something like thirty years at both venues in the past. Now that I was on my own it seemed appropriate to visit familiar places where there would be people I knew and could talk to. Good therapy, I thought, but after these enjoyable days the worst part was coming home with no-one there to talk about them to. I became determined that I'd eventually get used to the situation.

During the summer of 2010, my thoughts had regularly returned to the idea of driving the Oldsmobile across America, but I'd immediately put such thoughts out of my mind.

About that time I met Sue and George Darbyshire. Sue successfully races a vintage Morgan three-wheeler. I'd read about her achievements and I knew that George, her husband, was an ace mechanic.

We started talking about doing the USA trip together and although I warmed to the idea, I couldn't quite bring myself to starting up the Oldsmobile. The last time it ran was when Trevor and I drove it over to Prescott for a trial run after the re-build was finished. It didn't seem right to actually start the vehicle without Trevor being there. There was a certain technique to starting it and I couldn't imagine anyone else knowing the procedure. Perhaps I was subconsciously frightened that something would go wrong with the engine and then what would happen? Thoughts of selling the car occasionally went through my mind. Why own a car that I could not start and run myself without being dependent on other people? With so many conflicting thoughts racing through my head it was a difficult and confusing time for me.

Then I met Mark Riley. He had purchased my late father's Cooper-Norton and we'd seemed to hit it off straight away. One day he called in for a cup of tea as he was in the area and I happened to tell him about the trip that Trevor and I had been planning.

"I'll come with you," was his immediate response. I was flabbergasted.

"Don't be silly!" I retorted. "I don't know you and you don't know me."

I started telling him about people who, hardly knowing each other, form partnerships for long distance rallies and fall out dramatically during the event. I've even known of a few cases where co-drivers have completely walked out in some far-away place, even of husbands and wives falling out and ending up in the divorce court. I certainly didn't want to put myself in any situation of conflict – I'd need to know that I could get on well with whoever I was travelling with.

However, over the next few months I saw Mark, George and Sue at race events and got to know them well. So much so that we decided we could start talking together as a team with the possibility of crossing the USA with the Oldsmobile in 2013. It would, of course, depend on my raising sponsorship to cover all the costs.

I had booked to travel with my mother to Geelong for three months, starting December 2010. Previous trips to my hometown had been short and infrequent and I wanted to find out if I thought I could go back to Australia to live. In my mind, a week or two wasn't enough time for this so I'd settled on three months.

Although I'd escaped one of the coldest winters in England for years, after a couple of weeks I was ready to return home to the UK. But I persevered and after six weeks I started to enjoy myself and to feel that Geelong wasn't such an alien place after all. Perhaps I could live there, I decided, but I wasn't yet ready for such a dramatic change.

Thoughts about driving the Oldsmobile across the USA became more resolute during the three month sojourn. For the first time I convinced myself that it could be achieved, but only if I could somehow find the solution to covering the team's costs. The only negative factor appeared to be that, as I've previously said, I dislike intensely the actual procedure of trying to obtain sponsorship. But I also knew that if I really wanted to do this trip, I had to get on with the job. It appeared to me to be a chicken and egg situation. There was no point in making any arrangements without sponsorship funds in the pot, so I couldn't promise any of the team that the trip would really be on.

On returning to the UK in the spring of 2011, I finally set about the task of finding sponsorship. I had some luck with goods being supplied in kind, but the biggest chunk of expenses would involve accommodation, shipping and air fares so I needed a big lump sum to cover all that. No hotel chain offered any assistance with rooms, nor had any airline with flights, so I started to feel like a failure.

But at least my new team seemed to have confidence in me. George and Mark started looking at the Oldsmobile to familiarise themselves with its mechanical features. The first time it was started I felt nervous but once fired up she sounded healthy. As we had no MOT a road trip was out of the question, but we took her up and down the drive and she seemed to cope well.

George and Mark decided that before we took the car out on the road, the body should be lifted off to enable them to scrutinize the mechanics. We did this over a weekend, there were no visible faults and both George and Mark were now aware of how this ancient 1904 vehicle functioned. We made a list of all the jobs that needed doing and over the coming months they would all be accounted for.

Unfortunately, the team lived in widely differing locations, all some distance from my house, where the Olds is garaged. The Darbyshires and Mark all had extremely busy lives at work as well as in motorsport, competing on many weekends. I knew that to fit in a new project would be difficult for them.

Mark was able to spend a couple of weekends with the Olds and after it had passed the MOT test, we managed a few short trips of 20 or 30 miles. The car ran well once Mark had become familiar with the necessary fuel mixture adjustment to suit differing weather conditions. He'd also mastered the starting technique. Now, with just one short turn of the starting handle, the Olds would spring into life.

CHAPTER 7

THE TEAM COMES TOGETHER

The Oldsmobile seemed to be ready for its trip of a lifetime. I had a new team, all keen to travel coast to coast across the USA, but I still could not guarantee that the trip could be a reality. Sponsorship was still required.

The other members of the team could only be away for a maximum of five weeks, so I needed to modify the route and shorten the mileage to suit. Gary Hoonsbeen suggested that since our final destination was Daytona Beach we should leave from San Diego and keep south. I spent weeks studying every aspect of a modified route using Google maps. Instead of leaving from San Francisco, we would leave from Los Angeles and head east. But I didn't just want to go direct to Daytona Beach. As well as going via New Orleans I was keen to visit an American Indian reservation.

It was difficult, too, trying to organise an achievable daily mileage where accommodation was also available. As a comfortable speed in the Oldsmobile is a mere 25 mph, the maximum distance from one night's accommodation to the next had to be no more than 130 miles, which would need to exclude climbing mountains. Ascending steep roads might necessitate changing down to first gear, which would achieve little more than walking pace. In a modern car, an extra 20 or 30 miles wouldn't be a problem but in the Olds it would add more than an hour to our timetable. This would be too much for the Oldsmobile as without headlamps, we couldn't travel after sunset.

As the US is such a culturally diverse nation I wanted the opportunity to interact with as many people as possible. This would be difficult when driving all day and at one point I thought I might have to scrap my plan for travelling extensively through New Mexico's Zuni territory to see the Indian reservation, as there appeared to be no accommodation nearby. I persevered, and found an unexpected bonus – there was actually a guest house at the Zuni Reservation.

Spending so much time with the planning and getting excited about the route, I began to become disheartened about not being able to secure sponsorship.

Jim Carr, who I'd met eight years previously on the London to Sydney Marathon, visited me and over dinner we started talking about this increasing problem. A solution was in sight as Jim decided he could offer 50% of my estimated figure. It was now up to me to find the other 50%. I thought long and hard, eventually deciding that my Pilbeam single-seater racing car, in which I'd scored many wins and even outright hillclimb records, had finally to be sold. Since I was no longer able to afford to compete, I had originally intended to use the money from the sale as my pension. Rash decision or not, I decided to use my 'pension' to finance 50% of the trip. That, in my view, would at least show commitment.

There was already somebody interested in buying the Pilbeam, so I finally had to say goodbye to it. It was upsetting to watch my racing car being towed out of my drive on someone else's trailer. I felt as if part of my life, and my achievements, were disappearing forever. Tears streamed down my face. But then, I thought, all of the memories are still there; the trophies, the record books and the photographs. All that was leaving was a mechanical object, which was going to be driven again in competition rather than sitting in my garage, unused and deteriorating.

Within a couple of months, all the necessary sponsorship money had been secured and deposited in the bank. The new challenge was now a reality. The costs could be met. The feeling was unbelievable!

Although it was over a year to the start and still a considerable amount of work and planning to do, I could at least feel confident knowing that now it really was going to happen.

The route planning was complete and I was confident that all the daily mileages, with the longest at 130 miles, could be achieved. Where I perceived there would be mountains to climb, which would mean first gear driving, the mileage was relatively short. There would be just a few days in Arizona and New Mexico of around 60 miles each.

Several people had asked how I knew whether the roads I'd chosen would be suitable for the Oldsmobile and suggested I should travel to the USA for a reconnaissance trip. In reality, I didn't know. But the costs for another trip in a modern hire car would certainly add considerably to my budget and I didn't want to have to raise any more money. Deep down, I probably wanted to visit the US aboard the Oldsmobile as a virgin traveller. It wouldn't feel as adventurous if I'd travelled the route beforehand in a modern car.

Six months before we were due to leave the UK, our team members Sue and George had to abandon plans for the trip. George had recently set up his own business and became so inundated with work that he couldn't afford the time away. We soon welcomed a new member, Nick Cooper. Nick was a mechanic and friend of Mark, who was confident about Nick's mechanical abilities. That was good enough recommendation for me.

We decided to buy a fully enclosed trailer in which to ship the Oldsmobile to the USA. All the tools and spare parts could then be carried every day as well as providing a lock-up garage for the Oldsmobile every night. Months before the Olds was due to be shipped out, we started to organise the trailer so that anything required could be easily located. A particularly important feature as far as Nick and Mark were concerned was the location of the portable stove and kettle for their innumerable daily cups of tea.

Just four months before our departure we gained an unexpected fourth team member when Jim Carr, our 50% sponsor, decided he'd travel with us for the entire trip. He'd already arranged the support car needed to tow the trailer and transport the team members who weren't travelling with me in the Oldsmobile. A contact in Phoenix would hire us a Chrysler Voyager, which was meant to be 10 years old but turned out to be more than twenty but at least it was fitted with a tow-bar! This would mean flying into Phoenix, then driving the 350 miles to Los Angeles before picking up the Oldsmobile from the docks. Several friends voiced their concerns about using a Chrysler as its reputation for reliability was regarded as less than first class, but Jim insisted it would be OK.

At about this time I'd started to become concerned about the first day's drive from Los Angeles to Palm Springs. I suspected the heavy urban traffic of Los Angeles might be challenging for both the Oldsmobile and its driver and wondered if there was an alternative road to the Interstate. There wasn't, and anyway it would be illegal – not to mention dangerous – to travel in such a slow vehicle on the Interstate, where the minimum speed is 55 mph.

After another look at the maps I chose to leave from Oceanside, 83 miles south of Los Angeles, then head east to Julian, a former mining town more than 4,200 feet above sea-level. The journey was just 65 miles, a relatively short first day but at that altitude, one that would certainly be challenging for the Oldsmobile. On the map it appeared to be achievable but we wouldn't really know that until the day came.

I'd thought that after having sorted out the sponsorship to finance the trip, my anxiety levels would decrease. Not so. Now, I began to be concerned over the route I'd chosen. How would I know if the Oldsmobile was able to climb steep, mountainous roads? My experience in such a situation was non-existent. The only solution was to wait and see.

Towards the end of 2012, as a shake-down for its epic journey, Mark and I decided to give the Olds another run on the London to Brighton. Although we had been on short road runs during the summer months, the 62 mile Brighton Run is fairly challenging and although Trevor and I had participated twice in the UK's premier veteran event, I wanted to know how the Oldsmobile would fare following its total rebuild.

I was hopeful that the weather would be pleasant and mild, even though the Met Office had forecast torrential downpours in the south of England until mid-afternoon. Lined up alongside the Serpentine at 7.30 in the morning, perched on the Olds in the company of 449 veterans waiting for the start, it wasn't hard to realise that the Met Office were spot on for a change. The rain had been pelting down for hours and I was regretting I'd even entered this prestigious event. But once the flag dropped and we were away through the sodden streets of London, thoughts of heavy rain seemed to disappear from my mind to be replaced by a mental picture of Brighton's Madeira Drive. I had told Mark that the event is not a race but more of a tour, and although my competitive spirit had come to the fore in previous years, this time I would take it easy and look after the Olds for its forthcoming USA trip.

Rather like the green light on a hillclimb startline, when a Union Jack is dropped it sparks off something in me and from Hyde Park to Brighton we overtook every veteran car possible. Over wet roads, through traffic jams and even across red lights (when directed by the police), the Olds surged on. In spite of the inclement weather, spectators lined almost the entire 62 mile route waving and shouting encouragement to every chugging veteran. The party atmosphere was impossible to resist and we couldn't help but wave back. Near Redhill, the road was flooded and the water level just about reached the axles. We gently drove through while a kind lady, dressed in waterproofs and wellington boots, directed us to the shallowest part. After the compulsory stop at Crawley the rain eased and when I started to shiver, I realised my waterproofs had not lived up to their name – my five layers of clothing were wet through.

The Olds negotiated the undulating country roads and leapt up the steep Sussex hills with ease, running considerably better than before its rebuild with only the last hill before Brighton requiring a change to low gear.

Just over four hours after starting out we arrived at the ceremonial finish on Madeira Drive in sunshine and under blue skies. It had been a most challenging Brighton Run, but one of my most enjoyable. I was pleased that I'd had the opportunity of driving a veteran in such adverse conditions. At last, I was really impressed with the performance of this 1904 Curved Dash Oldsmobile and realised that it was indeed ready for its trip of a lifetime.

Trevor and Joy arriving at Crawley during the 2006 London to Brighton Veteran Car Run.

At Crawley.

Trevor lifting the engine out of the chassis.

Joy with the piston, conrod and cylinder.

Gary Hoonsbeen and Joy in Minneapolis with Gary's 1904 Oldsmobile chassis.

Trevor with the massive flywheel.

The chassis painted awaiting its engine.

Mark enlarging the hole in the tow-bar of the support vehicle.

Mark oiling all the moving parts before the start of the epic journey.

Mark and Joy ready to start from Oceanside Pier, California.

Starting to climb on the way to Julian, Caifornia.

We pass a vintage motorist in a Model A Ford.

Leaving Julian with Bill and Anne Otterman in their 1903 Oldsmobile.

Joy in the Algodones sand dunes.

Mark and Joy amazed at the vastness of the Algodones sand dunes.

A different type of Californian desert.

Time for refreshments.

The long straight road.

Off-roading to avoid the Interstate.

More off-roading through a creek bed.

CHAPTER 8

READY TO GO

When asked the question, as I often was, I became so used to saying that the USA trip was 'not until next year', that it still seemed like forever away.

Then January 1st, 2013 arrived and I was at a Vintage Sports Car Club new years' day pub-meet. I was asked the usual question and replied, with sudden realisation, that it was all going to happen in just a few months.

I was booked to fly out of the UK at the beginning of April, but the Oldsmobile was scheduled to leave by container at the beginning of February, which would be in just over a month's time.

There was a flurry to get the trailer sorted out with the tools and spare parts – not to mention the kettle and portable stove – all positioned for easy access. To a non-tea drinker like myself it looked like my two team members had packed enough teabags to cater for the entire population of the USA. I couldn't imagine that so much tea could be drunk in just five weeks.

After the trailer had been packed with all this equipment – and of course the Oldsmobile itself – we were ready for notification of the shipping departure date. The shipping schedules had to be arranged at short notice and owing to Nick and Mark's busy working lives, it was difficult to find a date to deliver the Olds to the docks. Eventually one was arranged and the three of us headed to Thamesport on a cold winter's morning, hoping that the forecast snow would fail to arrive. We were lucky weather-wise, but when we arrived at the docks we discovered that the trailer was two inches too wide for the container. Although dimensions had been discussed and finalised, I still can't understand what went wrong. We had to bring the whole lot back home again while the shipping agent set about finding another way to accommodate it.

My anxieties were starting to rise again and I began to worry that we might not be able to start this trip after all. After so many hours during the long build-up with negative feelings, I'd really thought that from now on it would be all systems go. How wrong I was.

Back home again with the car and everything else packed, all I could do was wait for news from the shipping agent. I'd heard rumours that after its arrival in the US, the Customs might hold back a car for no apparent reason. I started to feel extremely anxious as our entire daily plans for the trip including accommodation, for which deposits had been taken, had already been organised.

There was now a strong possibility that the ship would leave from Southampton, which was considerably closer to Mark's Somerset base than Thamesport. He decided to take the trailer and contents to his home, where I would meet him for the delivery trip.

We were eventually notified that the trailer would be shipped on a flat rack, a container with front and back doors but no side walls. The cost would be double, the trailer would need to be covered with tarpaulins and the container ship would in fact leave from Thamesport, not Southampton. That left us with a logistical problem. Fortunately I have friends in Wiltshire so I arranged to leave my road car at their place, which was on Mark's route to Thamesport.

I'd need to leave home at 6.00am, allowing two hours to get to Wiltshire, but as snow was forecast I thought it would be wiser to leave earlier. The Met Office report was correct. My car was covered in about four inches of snow and unaware of what road conditions would be like through Gloucestershire and Wiltshire, I wasn't confident about meeting Mark at 8.00am. I needn't have worried. Most of the snow had fallen in my own area and although I arrived at our meeting place a few minutes late, Mark was only just arriving.

We arrived at Thamesport on time at 11.00am. I was confident that the loading procedure would not take more than an hour. More snow had been predicted for my return journey and I didn't look forward to being on the road in the dark and in snow.

I was to be disappointed. We were kept hanging about for a couple of hours with nothing apparently happening and couldn't work out what the delay was. Eventually we found out that the flat-rack container that had been delivered was the wrong type. The front and rear doors opened inwards, not outwards, which meant that the trailer and its contents had to be loaded from the side using a fork-lift. Fair enough, we thought. However, no-one could give the packers the authority to do this. Despite the fact that I was the owner of the cargo, only the shipping agent had the requisite authority and none of his representatives was present. The packers, we were told, were waiting for either an email or a phone call for permission to load.

Mark and I waited until about 2.00pm, when I phoned the agent to be told that everything was now under control and an email had been sent. We still continued to wait and I started to become concerned about my forthcoming trip back across the Cotswolds. Visions of snowdrifts loomed, with the possibility of being stranded in some remote area.

After another phone call to the agent, who seemed surprised that things hadn't yet been sorted out, the trailer was eventually loaded. By 4.00pm, five hours after we'd arrived, we finally left Thamesport.

It was 10.00pm by the time I arrived home and for once I was pleased that the Met Office had got it wrong – I hadn't seen a single flake of snow.

The next step would be to pack my suitcase, fly to the USA and pick up the trailer at Long Beach, California on April 8th. Suddenly, the trip that had been in my mind for nearly six years was at last becoming a reality. There was no turning back now. The car was on its way and, in a matter of weeks, I would be too.

CHAPTER 9

WE ARE ON OUR WAY

Enquiring about flights to Phoenix, where we had to pick up the Chrysler Voyager support car, we found there were two options – a direct flight from Heathrow or one via Minneapolis. Minneapolis is the home of CDO Club founder Gary Hoonsbeen who, as I mentioned, had always been supportive of our trip as he had driven his 1902 Curved Dash Olds from coast to coast back in 1985.

There would be no extra cost to stop over for the night, so I arranged a 24-hour break in order to catch up with Gary. It was a diversion I was really looking forward to.

The night before flying out of the UK, Andrew Riley, owner of prestigious Cotswolds restaurant Russells of Broadway, offered to put on a fish and chip and champagne supper to help raise funds for Cancer Research UK, the charity I'd become involved with. I'd invited people I knew and that had shown interest in our USA trip. The food was good, everyone appeared to enjoy themselves and I felt that chatting to people who were aware of the significance of the forthcoming challenge would be a fitting way to spend my last evening.

After an early start at 7.00am to drive to Heathrow airport, it wasn't until the plane had taken off that I could sit back and relax. We were on our way and would leave Oceanside, California in the Oldsmobile in just one week's time. After planning and talking about the trip for the previous seven years, it still felt unreal that it was about to begin.

Gary and his wife Nancy entertained us well. I was travelling with Jim Carr, our part-sponsor, who was enthralled to view Gary's collection of veteran cars which included three Oldsmobiles, a 1909 Reo, a Stanley Steamer just undergoing a rebuild and a Cadillac. But what fascinated me more was the impressive pipe organ that Gary had installed in an enormous room under his house. I could have listened to the music all day. It would be nice, I felt, to live not too far from Gary as I could happily while away many hours there in his company.

The weather had been cold in England before we left, but in Minneapolis the temperatures were just above freezing and snow was stacked high at the side of the roads. So it seemed amazing that after the three hour flight to Phoenix the following day, the temperature was about 90°F – quite a contrast.

After Phoenix, we headed off on the day's drive to Los Angeles in the ageing Chrysler support car. Arrangements had been made to pick up the trailer with the Oldsmobile from the shipping agent the following morning. I'd been informed that the cargo had arrived about two weeks previously and was relieved that US Customs had allowed the Olds, tools and spares (including the teabags) into the country without any problems. So far, everything was going to plan. I hoped that the trailer, and particularly the Olds, hadn't suffered any damage during transit across the Atlantic and through the Panama Canal. In just 24 hours, I would have the answers.

It's a pity one wastes time and energy feeling negative. We arrived at the shipping agent's premises on the Monday morning to find the trailer, together with the Olds, stored in a warehouse, safe and sound and looking ready for the trip. Then we hit a problem.

We'd brought our UK towball to suit our British manufactured trailer, as standard American towballs are a different size. But when Jim went to fit it he found that the hole in the Chrysler's towing bracket was too small. We located a shop that sold towing equipment. They had tow-balls listed which would resolve our difficulties, but none was available for at least three weeks. The next idea was to find a back-street garage with suitable equipment to drill a bigger hole, but not knowing the district we couldn't locate one. The only option was to wait for Mark and Nick to arrive the following afternoon.

I'm sure that after being picked up at LA airport our two jet-lagged team members were looking forward to spending their first day relaxing by a swimming pool, beer in hand, enjoying the sun. But no. As soon as we'd picked them up it was back to the shipping agent and straight to work! Brian and Sevino of Southern Counties Express kindly lent us gas cutting equipment and Mark appeared to be in his element. In a short time he had the job completed and with the hole in the towing bracket now the correct diameter and the trailer hitched up and towing well, we were all set to drive for the following morning's 83 mile journey to Oceanside.

The hotel we were booked into was some five miles from the start venue, Oceanside Pier, which I was keen to visit. 1,942 feet in length, Oceanside Pier is the longest wooden pier along the entire US West Coast. It was the fifth replacement since the original pier was first built in 1888, its successors all having been destroyed by storms. During the planning stages I'd been attracted to Oceanside because I'd thought the pier's location on the Pacific Ocean would make an ideal backdrop for photographs. Once we settled into the Hotel outside Oceanside, checked the trailer, the Oldsmobile and of course made the obligatory cups of tea, I was keen to visit the start venue. My first view of the site confirmed my first assessment. The Pier looked spectacular – an absolutely ideal place to start our challenging trip.

It was easy to see that Mark doesn't live near the seaside. !mmediately, he'd taken off his shoes and went paddling in the Pacific Ocean while Nick and I went for a stroll along the pier. I was amazed at the number of people dangling fishing lines over the railings and hauling in vast numbers of fish. This was clearly a rich source of fresh fish, mackerel as I later discovered, for the local markets and restaurants. I also learned that although licences are required to fish along the coast they were not necessary for the Pier, which explained the large numbers of fishermen. Perhaps we, too, should have thrown a line over the side and cooked our own meal that day! Next time, perhaps ...

Back at the hotel, Mark was keen to start up the Oldsmobile after its long journey from England. The battery was almost flat but there was still enough power to start the car. She sprung into life almost immediately but we were a bit concerned about the different type of fuel that we had to use in the US. The ethanol content was different to fuel available in the UK and single-cylinder, 109 year old veterans were not used to the modern fuel mixture. After several test drives up the road and mixture adjustments on the carburettor, Mark started to feel a bit more relaxed. The battery was recharged overnight in the hotel room and after a test run next day, we all felt much more comfortable now that the Olds had adapted to its new fuel.

I didn't want to go out and just drive the Olds up the road and refused the opportunity. I knew I should get some experience of driving on the 'wrong' side, but I just couldn't bring myself to do it, deciding to wait until the actual start on Saturday.

I'm confessing it now, but I've always had hang-ups about driving the Olds. It all started back in 2006, when I first purchased her, but with a little bit of experience I always managed to overcome the problem. After periods of not driving the car the anxieties always re-emerge, and no matter what I say to myself they never fully disappear. Only five months earlier I'd driven on the Brighton Run and the uneasiness had vanished as soon as the Union Jack was dropped. I couldn't figure out why just a few months without driving the Oldsmobile could completely change my mental attitude towards it but I couldn't be persuaded, under any circumstances, to get on the driving seat. The way I finally managed my mental state was by telling myself that at the actual start, at 8.00am on April 13th, there was no alternative – no let-out, I just had to get on with it. After all, I'd managed the Oldsmobile in the past without a problem and this was no different. I hoped I was right!

Another concern was the route for our first day. We would start at sea-level and in just 65 miles we'd be 4,250 feet above it. I'd never had any experience with my Oldsmobile over mountains and whilst planning the route with the Google maps I was well aware there would be steep climbs on our first day. Steep climbs in a century old, single cylinder, two-speed Oldsmobile mean that when it's necessary to change down to the lower gear, you're at mere walking pace. I wasn't really aware of how much lower gear work there would be on the first day. I persuaded the rest of the team that we should travel over half the route in the support car the day before. I wasn't sure how that would help my anxiety but after seeing the steep climbs, I realised that the first day was certainly going to be extremely challenging.

And then determination took over. I didn't want to fail at this point – Trevor was watching me. And he wasn't used to dealing with a feeble-minded female.

DAY 1

Saturday 13th April
Oceanside to Julian, California

For our first day of travel it was going to be an early 8.00am start. I'd originally envisaged Oceanside as a small seaside town that we'd be able to leave by driving for a short distance along Mission Avenue to Highway 76, before being immediately in the countryside. On arrival several days earlier I'd been surprised at just how big the city was, the urban sprawl extending for miles along our route with countless traffic lights, so I wanted to try and avoid the Saturday morning commuter traffic as much as possible. Oceanside population had grown at a phenomenal rate. Back in 1888 the population was approximately 1,000 and at the 2010 census the population had increased to 183,095.

Oceanside had started out as a mission run by the Franciscan Brothers in 1798 until it closed in the 1840s, by which time the area's advantages were common knowledge. It was the time when huge Mexican land grants were available in this part of southern California. Many large ranches were set up in the area and the seaside became the place to holiday, giving relief from the stifling inland heat.

Oceanside's development took off after WW2 when Camp Pendleton, the nation's largest Marine Corps base, was built and families from the armed forces moved into the area.

On arrival at the Pier just after 7.00am to prepare for our start we were amazed at the number of people milling about, including television film crews.

No, they hadn't come to wave us off. It turned out they were there for the annual 'March for Babies' fundraising walk. None of the crews seemed remotely interested that we were about to drive a 109-year-old Oldsmobile over 3000 miles from Oceanside to the Atlantic coast. The walk was scheduled to start at 8.00am and we were instructed by the organisers to be out of the way before the walkers returned after their one stint around the block.

A couple of months earlier we'd contacted Mayor Jim Wood, Oceanside's elected Mayor, who had offered to wave us off from the Pier. Originally in the police force, Jim's dry sense of humour had me laughing immediately. He went over to ask the TV reporters to film the start of our epic journey but they had other things on their agenda. "Never mind," I told him. "At least we have our own film crew, David Winstanley and his assistant Eni."

I'd been expecting a nice sunny morning for our start by the pier but it felt chilly, with damp mist in the air. I had to search through my suitcase to find a sweater to keep warm. Travelling in the Oldsmobile with no protection from the elements, it's essential to have all types of clothing readily available for unexpected weather conditions.

8 o'clock struck and it was time to leave. We collected a bucket of water from the Pacific Ocean and poured it over the rear wheels – on arrival at the Atlantic we would be dipping the front wheels into the ocean. Nick had brought a large Union Jack from England and we'd bought an American Stars and Stripes flag to match. We erected one on each side of the Oldsmobile.

Mayor Jim wished us well, Mark and I waved goodbye and with Oceanside Pier in the background, we set off on this damp, misty morning. I kept reminding myself that unlike in Britain and Australia, where I was more accustomed to driving, I must drive on the right-hand side of the road.

There was a steep rise from the beach front to the main road, where I had to turn left. I'd rehearsed in my mind how to cross the traffic lanes. I certainly didn't want to end up on the wrong side after travelling such a short distance from the start. I managed to navigate the Olds on to the far side of the road before the right turn onto Mission Avenue, where we'd arranged to meet the support crew and remove the flags which were far too big to have fluttering about our heads for the whole trip.

Nick and Jim with the support car and trailer had got caught up with the walkers and it seemed like forever before we saw them turn the corner. I just wanted to get on with driving and not waste any time. I was probably still anxious about my ability to drive on such a challenging day after a virtually sleepless night, which had hardly contributed to my sense of well-being.

Once under way my timing for traffic lights was abysmal. At virtually every junction, it seemed, they changed to red just before the Oldsmobile arrived. US traffic lights are different from those in the UK in that they change directly from green to red and back again, with no amber warning in between. With the Oldsmobile's brakes not as efficient as a modern car's I needed more space to stop and had to concentrate hard, trying to anticipate just when the lights were about to change. This first morning my judgement was not too accurate and I ran at least one red light. Fortunately there was no traffic coming in either direction so rather than braking hard, it was easier to stay committed and keep rolling.

After about 40 minutes we joined Highway 76 and headed for the mountains. There was considerable traffic and when the road became a single carriageway and started climbing, Mark had to keep looking behind to see if there was much of a build-up. As soon as there were about five cars I pulled over to the shoulder to let them pass. If the shoulder was not wide enough I pulled off into a convenient road or driveway –

when one could be found. At least the Californian drivers seemed to be tolerant of our slow vehicle and nearly everyone waved in a friendly manner, many taking photographs as they passed. Several even pulled up on the side of the road ahead so they could film us or take photographs. We always waved for them, too.

It soon became obvious that there was a Harley Davidson event taking place in the mountains. Hundreds overtook us, every rider giving a horizontal wave as the Harleys swept by, each machine emitting its characteristic deep, throbbing exhaust note.

When the road started to climb I was impressed by the way the Oldsmobile was pulling in high gear without losing much speed. The inclines weren't that steep to start with and as it was springtime, all the vegetation was green and bushes with bright red flowers lined the side of the road. After we'd passed through Palo Indian reservation, the greenery gave way to a massive development of Casino, Hotel and retail outlets; quite a contrast to what I was expecting. It reminded me of parts of Australia, where magnificent forests have been lost to massive concrete developments.

Suddenly, we were surrounded by the most wonderful citrus aroma and I was immediately aware of one of the advantages of not being confined in a box-like modern car with controlled atmosphere. Here on the Oldsmobile, we could experience all the natural fragrances as we drove through an orange grove.

The road became much steeper and narrower as it climbed through the forests. It wasn't long before I had to change down to first gear and keep to a steady 8 or 9 miles an hour. Nick had fitted a whistle on the end of the radiator's overflow pipe to signal when the water was boiling. After about fifteen minutes of steep climbing we noticed the support car waiting in a lay-by. This was a perfect opportunity to rest the Olds for a while to enable it to cool down and for Mark to indulge in his much needed cup of tea. Fortunately the kettle was already boiling so he didn't have to wait long.

We were joined by one of the Harley riders. He'd been photographing us at different points as we climbed and was rather surprised to learn that we were driving all the way to Daytona Beach. He confirmed that there was indeed a Harley event on and that some of the riders would be at Lake Henshaw, where we'd intended to stop for lunch.

We stayed in first gear for about 40 minutes until arriving at the Lake Henshaw plateau. I'd estimated our arrival time to be at least 2.00pm. It was, in fact, only mid-day and I was starting to be very impressed with my Oldsmobile and Trevor's rebuild.

David Winstanley had heard that Lake Henshaw's café had won awards for its chilli dishes and was keen to film me eating one of them. I usually only have a small sandwich for lunch so he filmed me ordering the chilli then tasting it, after which he took over and finished it – which, needless to say, was not recorded on film!

The café appeared to be a popular weekend venue. With the majority of tables filled with Harley riders I could see only one that was vacant.

We were now 2,723 feet above sea-level, with almost 2,000 feet still to climb. After an hour's break it was time to move on again for the final 18 miles. The ascent was surprisingly gradual and the Olds pulled well. At a crossroads a 1930s Model A Ford pulled up beside us.

"Why don't you buy a more modern car?" the driver called out.

"Sorry," I countered, "I can't afford one!"

Several miles before Julian, our destination for the day, the road became steep and once again it was into low gear, although only for about five minutes. Soon we arrived in Julian and it was only 3.00pm. I'd reckoned on 6.00pm being the arrival time, so I really had underestimated the Oldsmobile's abilities. I became quite emotional when we pulled up in front of the Gold Rush Hotel, our overnight accommodation after our first and most challenging day on the road. Tourists appeared from nowhere to gaze at the Olds. When we answered their question, "Are you here for a car show?" we were amused by their looks of amazement at our reply: "No, we're driving to Daytona Beach and just passing through."

Julian experienced a gold rush in the 1870s. After a former slave had found gold, it quickly became a tent city. The rush was short-lived but while the mining flourished, James Madison had brought a wagonload of young apple trees up into the mountains and the fruit trees flourished in the clear, fresh air. Apples are still a big product in Julian, many of them being used to make the world-famous Julian apple pies. Not surprisingly, all my team members were keen to scamper off in search of them before we moved on.

65 miles.

DAY 2

Sunday 14th April
Julian to Brawley, California

It was a disappointing start to the day as I looked out of my hotel room window just after 7.00am. The fog was so thick I could barely see more than a few feet across the street. It certainly wasn't the time to put away the winter woollies, in fact I needed to find a few more.

The hotel had been recently refurbished using Victorian style antique furniture similar to when it first opened in 1890. I'd never seen such a high bed and had to put my suitcase on the floor to get in and out, but at least the room had a small en-suite shower to take it into the 21st century.

Included in the price was a traditional breakfast for which the hotel is renowned, which included Queen Oats Granola. None of us was familiar with such American delicacies and as I don't usually eat a large breakfast, I had to forgo most of the courses. Just as we were finishing breakfast we were joined by fellow Curved Dash Oldsmobile owners Bill and Anne Ottemann, who had brought along their 1902 model. Bill had contacted me several months before and although he had a previous commitment on day one of our trip, he'd offered to meet us in Julian and accompany us to Brawley, our next night stop.

Anne felt cold on this foggy day and we sat by a wood fire in the hotel foyer to thaw out. After poking my head out of the front door I wasn't relishing the idea of driving the Oldsmobile in these conditions.

Out in the street, Mark and Nick had started the Olds and prepared it for its second day of driving. With the two Oldsmobiles parked together it wasn't long before the crowds were milling about to watch our departure. I'm sure they all thought we were completely bonkers to drive our open horseless carriages in such cold weather. As Bill was familiar with the route to Brawley, I was happy for him to lead in his slightly older vehicle. Leaving Julian we were climbing again, although not for long. The descent soon started on a narrow, curving road wending its way through dense oak forests.

The previous day my anxieties had vanished after the Olds had proved able to climb steep mountain roads, but today I was concerned about the efficiency of the two rear brakes. Would I be able to control the speed to a manageable level as we descended? Once we'd joined a wider road the downward gradient became more gradual. So far the brakes had given no indication that they would fail and my confidence started to rise.

Before long we'd left the dense forest behind and wound our way down through craggy, ochre coloured mountains. The sun was now shining brightly with not a cloud overhead. I stopped to let some traffic past and looked back to see clouds still lingering over the mountain forest.

In a few miles, after dropping to 2,000 feet, the roads suddenly became straight. It almost seemed unbelievable that in a couple of hours we'd passed from cold, damp weather to the hot and sunny Anza-Borrego Desert.

The surrounding pink hue gave way to a sandy colour and plants became sparser. We noticed sand or dust clouds in the distance, then discovered that this area is popular with 4x4 adventurers who have over 500 miles of dirt roads to keep them occupied.

After the rains, the area can be covered with a myriad of wild flowers attracting hundreds of visitors. I kept noticing a spindly looking plant, several feet high with a bright red flower, which looked out of place in the desert. Anne explained it was called Ocotillo which for much of the year looks like a large, spiny dead stick, but close observation revealed egg-shaped leaves. Apparently, these grow after rain and may remain for weeks, or even months, with the bright crimson flowers appearing at the tip of each mature stem. It was now mid-April, so the large number of these flowers would indicate a fairly recent rainfall.

By now Mark had started to hanker after a cup of tea. In the distance, down the long straight road, I thought I could see the support team waiting. Expecting David to be filming the two Oldsmobiles approaching, about a half a mile before we arrived I did an overtaking move on the Ottemann's Olds which I thought would make good footage. But David wasn't there filming and my bold move was for nothing, which left me rather embarrassed and open to accusations of showing off.

But the kettle was boiling so the timing was perfect. Mark was relieved and our two American friends, Bill and Anne, had the opportunity of experiencing a cup of good English tea, a beverage to which they were unaccustomed.

Sitting on the seat of the Oldsmobile ready for the next stage, I began to feel the heat and started shedding layers of clothing. The temperature had risen to somewhere near 90°F, quite a contrast to when we left Julian not too many hours before.

It was an easy run now. A relatively straight road, then right on to the Highway 86 dual carriageway just over twenty miles from Brawley and our night's stop. The traffic density began to increase and it was clear that the relative isolation we'd enjoyed earlier was over. We were in agricultural and cattle country, serviced by the vast irrigation canals and green paddocks now visible on both sides of the road.

Having descended from 4,235 feet we were at present below sea level, for Brawley is an amazing 112 feet below the level of the ocean.

We passed near to Salton Sea, one of the world's largest inland seas and at 227 feet below sea level, one of the lowest spots on earth. Salton Sea first appeared in 1905, when high spring flooding on the Colorado River crashed the canal gates leading into the developing Imperial Valley. For the next 18 months the entire volume of the Colorado River rushed downwards into the Salton Trough. By the time engineers were finally able to stem the flow two years later, the 45 mile long and 20 mile wide Salton Sea had been created. Because it has no outflow and is now fed only by agricultural run-off, the sea's salinity level increases every year. At the moment it is saltier than sea-water, resulting in very few species of fish being able to survive.

I was advised not to bother to visit this once prosperous tourist and wildlife area as the smell of accumulated algae and bacteria is almost unbearable.

The town of Brawley, with its population of 25,000, is flat and spread out with wide streets, so the motel we were booked into was easily found.

I was surprised to find that it was still only 2.30pm – I was becoming even more impressed with my Oldsmobile.

The sun was hot and I looked for some shade, but there was just one tree. Workmen were laying bitumen throughout the Motel's grounds and we needed to wait until it was set, we were told, before we could park near our rooms.

Fortunately the motel had its own air-conditioned restaurant and bar, so we quickly made our way there to get out of the heat of the sun and spend a little more time with Bill and Anne Ottemann.

Travelling in the company of another Oldsmobile for the day had been enjoyable and to drive through such contrasting terrain added another interesting dimension to our trip.

75 miles.

DAY 3

Monday 15th April
Brawley to Quartzsite, Arizona

Sunshine and a bright blue sky greeted us on day three but as I sat on the Oldsmobile seat just after 9.00am, waiting to leave, I started to question the sanity of the challenge I was putting us all through. It suddenly seemed like a daft idea, driving a 109-year-old vehicle from coast to coast for almost 3,000 miles – and for what?

David Winstanley's comment didn't help my confidence. He pointed out that by day three of our trip we'd travelled less than 150 miles, so it would feel like forever before we got to 3000 miles.

"I take one day at a time," I told him, "and so far we've achieved exactly what was planned."

He ended up by agreeing and decided not to mention the subject of overall mileage again until we reached the finish.

So Mark and I headed off through the almost deserted streets of Brawley. It wasn't long before we were travelling through highly irrigated agriculture areas, laid out in a grid system with different crops on each plot. The vegetation seemed to attract a variety of insects. If I hadn't already eaten breakfast, there would have been plenty of insects to digest as they crashed into our faces and landed on our clothes.

I decided that I wouldn't like to be a farmer in this part of the country. It looked to me like a hard life in small farm houses with no visible signs of wealth.

About fifteen miles into our journey, heading north on Highway 78, we crossed a canal about twenty feet wide. That was the end of the agriculture and greenery – and, fortunately, the insects. Looking down, I found my shirt covered in dead, green ones.

Now the terrain became desert-like and dotted with stunted bushes. We noticed a few farms in the distance and got the impression that it would be difficult to eke out a living in this dry, sparsely populated area.

During the route planning stages back in the UK I'd reached the conclusion that today's route would be quite monotonous; a relatively straight, flat road with little interesting landscape to hold our attention. I was wrong. Travelling through the desert offered much diversity, with the flat sections followed by rises through rocky crevices. We could see the craggy Chocolate Mountains in the distance to our right; such a contrast to the damp, forested mountains we'd descended the previous day. It was as if we'd been travelling in two different countries.

The Olds was chuff-chuffing along healthily, seemingly enjoying the dry environment. She was pulling well up the gentle inclines too, without losing much speed.

Then suddenly, to our utter surprise, the environment swiftly changed. We were surrounded by sand-dunes and no vegetation, almost as if we were driving along the coast. It was eerie, we felt isolated and with a slight breeze blowing I started to feel concerned that we could end up stranded in a moving dune. We noticed our film crew up ahead and I pulled in beside their car. Being brought up on the Australian coast it appeared to me that if I wandered over one sand-dune, the rolling surf would be there to enjoy.

This area was called the Algodones Sand Dunes. Although no-one is entirely certain how they were created, the most popular theory is that the Dunes were formed from windblown beach sands of Lake Cahuilla, more than a hundred miles to the north-west where we'd stopped. The prevailing westerly and north-westerly winds carried the sand eastward from the old lake shore to their present location, which continues to migrate southeast by approximately one foot per year.

Nick and Jim arrived in the support car, which meant that after checking the Olds it was tea-time. However the stop was relatively short. I wanted to push on in case the wind became stronger, whipping up the sand, for none of us knew for how many miles along the road the dunes continued.

But after seven miles they disappeared and we were once again travelling through hilly, dry and desert-like conditions with more stunted trees on each side. Travelling through the rocky passes made me think of the western films I'd seen in my youth. I half expected a posse of cowboys to appear on horseback in pursuit of an Indian tribe.

Arriving in Palo Verde area near the Colorado River, the desert once more gave way to vast areas of irrigated agricultural land. The support team had found a pull-in on an old ox-bow bend in the river, shaded by tall trees, and we stopped for Mark's obligatory cup of tea and a short rest. Insects kept buzzing us so the rest period was short-lived and we soon hit the road again, the Oldsmobile springing into life with just half a turn of the starting handle.

We headed directly north until we reached Blythe, near the banks of the Colorado River and close to Interstate 10, one of the busy motorways we needed to avoid at all costs. Judging by the heavy machinery around it was clear that this area was heavily involved with cattle and agriculture. Although the Oldsmobile exhaust note is not loud, it was perhaps the slow beat that frightened the cows in the fields into a near stampede as they tried to escape from us.

It was easy to spot the Interstate in the distance as it was built-up quite high, so we turned right into a street which ran parallel to it, avoiding the massive trucks that we could see thundering past.

The back roads were relatively quiet with very little traffic but masses of intersections. This meant stop, back into first gear, then a change back into top, invariably just before arriving at the next intersection and having to start the procedure again. And all just as I was getting used to the wide, quiet roads away from urban areas! To make matters worse the road was full of pot-holes and although I tried my utmost, I couldn't avoid them all and the Oldsmobile would jolt severely as we hit them. I always apologised to her. About fifteen miles from our night's accommodation we entered Dome Rock Road. The surface was smooth, the terrain interesting and the Olds loved the dips and rises over the hilly countryside. Small bushes with glorious yellow flowers grew on both sides of the road, once again a total contrast to the flora of just a few miles back.

This had been our longest day so far and at 4.30pm, when we arrived at the Motel on the outskirts of Quartzsite, Arizona, the second state on our list, I felt somewhat relieved. The Olds' tiller steering had required all my concentration. When the road camber changes, which happens a lot, my concentration levels go up as well as the pressure on my arm. Unlike a steering wheel, where you can balance the pressure with both arms, with tiller steering the load all goes through one arm.

Quartzsite is a weird town. It has a summer population of 3,500, yet in the winter months this increases to over 250,000. It's a popular place for owners of recreational vehicles to escape the cold of the northern states and hence they've earned the name of 'snow-birds'. We could see acres of RV parks full of massive vehicles. I'm sure the electricity supply must increase considerably during the winter to supply their air-conditioning units.

Quartzsite is also the place to trade and buy rocks, gems, mineral specimens and fossils during the town's two-month-long gem show and swap-meet every January and February, together with an RV Show which attracts 750,000 visitors.

As Nick and Mark checked over the Oldsmobile and adjusted the chain tension after its day's run, they were joined by one of the local sheriffs. Cruising past, he'd spotted our ancient-looking car and curiosity got the better of him. He was genuinely interested in our challenge and spent more than an hour in our company. We were treated to a tour of his American 'muscle-car' which had a rear section like a jail, with seat removed so that prisoners could neither escape nor interfere with the driver. I was flabbergasted by the array of weapons stored in the boot, but then again I'm not accustomed to police methods in the USA, where guns are commonplace for either protection or apprehension of criminals.

The lack of a restaurant is one of the disadvantages of staying in cheap motels and we drove into town to find somewhere to eat. Months before, I'd read about the Quartzsite Yacht Club and became rather curious as to how such an establishment could exist right here in the Sonoran Desert, without water or a lake for miles.

The Club was started by Al Madden, whose investment company in California worked on a goldmine venture for clients in Quartzsite during the 1970s. Although his business venture was unsuccessful, Al spent a lot of time in the town and noticed that the local beer bar, 'The Jigsaw', was for sale. It was a small building of grey cement blocks and although it didn't look very attractive, he bought it with the help of his family.

Al, who was known for his great sense of humour, decided to change the name to 'The Yacht Club' with the motto 'Welcome aboard - long time no sea!' Membership of the Club was available for $10 and before long the numbers started to grow. There are now over 8,000 members from every state in the US as well as countries around the world. Nick and I couldn't resist the temptation and after hearing the spiel from the manager (most members, we were informed, do not own a yacht) we are now fully fledged members of the Quartzsite Yacht Club. So now that I have a membership card, baseball cap and T-shirt emblazoned with 'Quartzsite Yacht Club', I'm wondering whether my membership card will give me access to yacht clubs world-wide …

They cook a nice meal as well!

120 miles.

DAY 4

Tuesday 16th April
Quartzsite to Phoenix, Arizona

We left Quartzsite on time this morning. This was meant to be another 120 mile run heading east towards Phoenix, but the road I'd planned to avoid the Interstate was not serviceable anymore. Our sheriff friend had advised us of this the previous night and had showed us another route which meant heading north, adding at least another thirty miles or so to the route. This really would be a long day!

Nick was my passenger today and as we drove past the Quartzsite Yacht Club we saluted, to acknowledge our new yacht club membership.

Once clear of the town we turned left on to the Highway 96 dual carriageway and headed due north. Big trucks thundered past and many whopping great RVs also left Quartzsite with their snowbird occupants, most likely on the way home to the northern states to escape the hot desert sun.

After a few miles we turned right off the main highway and joined a narrow minor road. It was smooth, with no traffic and a stunning view of distant mountains. The sun was shining, the sky a clear blue and with the ochre coloured peaks in the distance it was like looking at a picture postcard. The view of the Bouse Hills and mountains was certainly spectacular. I'd been expecting flat, desert-like terrain instead of rises cutting through the rocky outcrops, but they were gradual enough for the Oldsmobile not to lose too much speed. For mile after mile the road curved, rose and fell. The air must have suited our horseless carriage as she purred every inch of the way without missing a beat. A variety of cacti, some with yellow flowers, some with red and many in the characteristic tall form seen in cowboy films, spread across the land. I was enjoying every minute of today's route, particularly the isolation and the lack of other traffic.

It was becoming increasingly obvious that cattle grazed on this part of the Arizona desert as every few miles along the road we came to a cattle grid. At first I didn't slow down too much, but not until the Oldsmobile wheels had hit it with a crash did I realise that there was a step from the grid to the road. From then on I slowed right down to walking pace. Nick was pleased, as he'd been trying to light a cigarette. I'm not sympathetic to smokers and didn't offer to stop. "Damn it," I muttered as I could see an approaching cattle grid with quite a big step. Nick whooped with delight, thinking I would finally stop. He pulled out his lighter but he never managed to get the cigarette alight as the breeze was too strong. I smiled to myself...

I'd never seen a coyote before until a scraggy looking specimen ran across in front of us. He must have a hard time trying to find food in this part of the Arizona desert.

Nick was becoming more and more concerned because, apart from his lack of nicotine, he hadn't joined in the morning's tea drinking ritual. Usually, the support car overtakes us within a few miles of leaving the hotel, then waits about ten miles up the road for the first stop to check the Olds. After another twenty miles it's time for oil and petrol and, of course, tea. But this morning we'd not set eyes on them or, for that matter, on the film crew. We began to think that they must have taken the wrong road.

Then just as we were entering Bouse, a small town of less than 1000 inhabitants, the support car came up behind us. Before long the kettle was boiling, tea-making was underway and we discovered they'd taken a different route.

Bouse was a mining town in the late nineteenth and early twentieth century. It was short-lived as the mines soon closed, although when the railroad arrived during the 1920s there was some employment available. We noticed many abandoned properties as we drove through, indicating much hardship for several of the residents.

What a contrast when we turned right onto highway 72, heading south-east. Heavy trucks passed us in both directions, buffeting the Olds and forcing me to grip the tiller with both hands. This, together with a gusting side wind, made this section less than enjoyable. The railway ran alongside the road, the heavily loaded trains continually blasting their loud hooters.

After twenty-five miles and more than an hour of driving along this fairly rough road, we came to an intersection and turned left to head north-east again. This certainly was turning into a zig-zag route, and all just to avoid the Interstate. Highway 60 was different, wide and well-maintained, and at the start we climbed a fairly steep, windy section. I wasn't sure whether the Olds would make it all the way in high gear, but just as I was contemplating changing down we reached the summit. In seven miles we'd reached Salome, turned right and were once again heading south-east, this time in the right direction for Phoenix. This road was a lot quieter and I started enjoying the solitude again, although there were several potholes to try and avoid. The stunted, sparse bushes and the grey colour of the sandy soil gave the impression that rainfall was a rare occurrence.

A bridge took us over the Interstate 10 and for a few minutes the cross-winds and air turbulence from the busy road buffeted the Olds about, causing me some difficulties as I struggled with the tiller. Beyond the bridge the road looked as if it hadn't been serviced for years – corrugations and potholes could not be avoided and I had to slow down to about 14 mph. This will only last for a mile or two, we thought, but in fact it continued for many miles before we had to turn onto an unmade road for a few more miles and then drive through a sort of creek. For a moment it seemed as if we were on an off-road rally stage in some remote area. Eventually, after some very deep, yet unavoidable holes the road became smoother and wider, almost as if it was new.

We stopped and checked the Oldsmobile. The mudguards had been rattling, the wooden wheels had taken a battering and I was worried about what might fall off this ancient vehicle on just its fourth day of travel. As it turned out nothing was wrong, she'd mastered all the adverse conditions with ease and was still sounding healthy, but we still had quite a number of miles to get under our belts before Phoenix and time was marching on. Without the luxury of headlamps, it was essential to arrive at our motel in the centre of Phoenix before sunset at 6.59pm and there were still over forty miles to go.

It was just after 5.00pm when we arrived at the start of the urban area. Not the ideal time, with commuter traffic rushing to get home to the outer suburbs. At least, or so I hoped, the majority of traffic would be travelling in the opposite direction to us. The double lane road was wide but I was surprised at just how many pot-holes there were, particularly at intersections. It was sometimes hard to avoid them in the heavy traffic. Several cars pulled alongside us when we pulled up for traffic lights and at intersections so that their passengers could take our photograph, which led to a number of three way conversations. Most had never seen a hundred-year-old vehicle before and were amazed that it was driven on the road at all, let alone for nearly three thousand miles.

Mile after mile of countless traffic lights made me wish that the motel would soon appear. We must have been lucky today; I would say that 90% of them were green, although I did run a couple of red lights.

Eventually we found the motel. The time on arrival in Phoenix was 6.30pm and the sun had just thirty minutes before the finish of its day. Perfect timing! It really had been a long driving day but I was delighted with it. Because we were unable to travel on the Interstate, we'd encountered an amazing variety of terrain, roads and conditions.

Nick and Mark then took over, thoroughly checking every accessible moving part on the Olds. Then, at last, it was time to find a restaurant.

160 miles.

DAY 5

Wednesday 17th April
Phoenix to Globe, Arizona

To avoid the early morning traffic we elected to leave the Motel in Phoenix after 9.30am, heading east through the populated urban area. The main road out of Phoenix was Interstate 10, which we needed to avoid at all costs.

It wasn't long before we came across the first set of traffic lights, in fact I could see lights at every intersection for quite some distance. This morning, my luck was not holding out. Almost every one turned red just when I was about to commit to driving through. "Why aren't they synchronized?" I muttered in frustration.

David offered to lead us in the film car as Nick and Jim were leaving later in the support car. Each car was equipped with a hand held GPS device which, even though they were set up to avoid the busy Interstate roads, all tried to navigate us to the nearest one. It was obvious that David was struggling to find a suitable route as every street we turned up was full of traffic lights, all about to turn red. We somehow found ourselves on a freeway, which seemed to be as busy as I imagine the interstate would be. It was pretty frightening as trucks and cars thundered past at high speed on every lane.

I could see David's car in the distance, pulled up on the shoulder. As I got closer I could see he was talking to the driver of a white van. I pulled up in front of them and heard the van driver's "Holy Moly!" This wasn't the first time we'd heard this expression from the lips of locals who'd just heard we were driving this 109-year-old car from coast to coast.

The van driver gave David precise instructions to get to Highway 60 and we headed off again, leaving the freeway at the next exit.

It was a relief to be off the freeway, but I was still yearning for quiet roads far away from the suburbs. We continued to follow David through the back streets until, to my utter surprise, we ended up in the Phoenix airport complex. How could we possibly end up bringing the Oldsmobile to one of USA's busiest airports? The traffic was at a virtual standstill and the number of people crossing the roads with suitcases in tow was mind-boggling. It was a stop/start situation and I was getting extremely fed up sitting in traffic queues as we inched past at least three terminals. There was apparently, said David later, no alternative route!

After yet more red traffic lights we eventually arrived on Highway 60. It had taken over two hours to clear the Phoenix suburbs. I was intrigued by the name of Superstition Freeway, as this highway was called. We'd previously seen Superstition Boulevard as we tried to find our way out of Phoenix and the mountain we could see on our left, east of Phoenix, was Superstition Mountain, so named because great treasure is believed to be hidden within it. Many adventurers have tried to find it without success and most have never returned. Better, we thought, to avoid this sacred place!

After we'd passed through Apache Junction and Gold Canyon, a former gold mining area, the traffic flow eased and I started to relax a little.

Highway 60's dual carriageway was quite busy but driving was not as hectic as in the city. The terrain was flat and dry with a few short bushes, saguaros and other varieties of cactus. On the horizon, we could see more mountains in the direction we were heading.

Fifteen or so miles out from Gold Canyon the highway divided into two, one heading south while the 60 headed east and started to climb gradually through sweeping bends. The surface was smooth and although there was a shoulder, I wasn't too keen to drive on it as it was corrugated to discourage its use. However if the traffic built up too much I would reluctantly move over.

My traffic spotter, Mark, had good cause to feel nervous in busy areas. He had to keep looking behind to check how close the traffic was getting and would warn me if a big truck was coming up.

Both Mark and I were amazed at how well the single-cylinder Olds was pulling up these inclines in the higher of its two gears, only dropping down to 18 mph. Whilst planning today's route many months earlier I'd envisaged that we'd be regularly changing down to the lower gear due to the altitude, but so far I'd been wrong. At this rate we'd arrive at our destination in Globe quite early as the total distance for the day was just 88 miles.

I was enjoying myself. The conditions were perfect and such a contrast from the busy urban areas. The Olds seemed to be purring like a kitten and my admiration for this amazing horseless carriage increased with each climb.

At one of our stops to replenish fuel and oil (and of course tea for Mark), Nick happened to mention that I would shortly have to negotiate a tunnel approximately a quarter of a mile long. I hadn't noticed this on the map beforehand and at first it gave me cause for a little anxiety. We arranged to stop before the tunnel at the nearest town, Superior, and switch on the bicycle lights we'd fitted to the rear of the Olds so that other drivers could see us easily.

As we climbed, sometimes through rocky outcrops, the view of the surrounding mountains was so stunning that I wanted to pull up just to soak in the atmosphere of this wonderful natural spectacle. But I had to remember that we were driving coast to coast. Time didn't allow for such luxuries, but at least we got to experience it all as we slowly drove through. As we climbed, the temperature started to drop and at one of the fuel/ tea stops I had to find a sweater and a waterproof jacket to protect myself from the chilly breeze. Just a few hours on from sweltering in the hot morning sun of Phoenix, we were now feeling cold.

As we entered Superior I noticed its elevation was 2,850 feet. The Olds had climbed over 1,700 feet without needing a change down into low gear.

It looked as if Superior had seen better days, presumably during its silver and copper mining period back in the early twentieth century, as many of its grand old buildings were now either abandoned or boarded up.

When we stopped to replenish the Oldsmobile's liquids and turn on the rear lights, I was rather surprised to see how sharply the road ahead appeared to rise. It looked challenging, and it was. After lulling myself into thinking that this would be a relatively easy day for my trusty carriage, its mettle – not to mention my own – was about to be tested again.

I managed to build up enough speed to change into the higher gear as we ascended and she seemed to remain at a constant 12 to 14 mph for about five miles. But with the tunnel in sight the road became steeper, the engine and transmission became hotter, the clutch started slipping and I fumbled as I changed down into the low gear, almost coming to a standstill. The entrance to the tunnel was the worst spot to make a mistake and I'd made one. It was a very frightening experience. Red rear cycle lights flashing, we crawled through the tunnel at walking pace while the road still climbed. The whistle Nick had fitted to the water overflow was shrilling loudly, telling us the poor old Olds was hot as hell – in fact boiling. As we exited the tunnel we noticed a pull-in and came to a grateful halt, so that the Olds and its occupants could rest. Fortunately, the rest of the team soon joined us and it was refreshments all round.

For another mile and a half we climbed, through steep, rocky cuttings in low gear while at times the road levelled out enough to build up speed for the higher gear. When we arrived at Top of The World, we'd reached 4,528 feet above sea-level – a 1,678 foot climb since we'd left Superior only nine miles back.

The inclines became gentler and we started to descend as we rolled into Miami, another silver and copper mining area and still operational. Now at 3,400 feet, we'd dropped over 1000 feet in a very short time. From then on it was an easy drive into Globe. Our hotel for the night was outside the town, perched high on a hill and offering the most spectacular mountain panorama imaginable.

Our landlord, Carl Williams, came out to view our unusual vehicle and invited us all into the bar to sample the local brew. After a few minutes some people arrived who were looking for us. They'd been following our progress via the internet and had driven over 200 miles just to see us pass by as we entered Globe. We'd arrived earlier than anticipated and with some careful detective work, they'd discovered our residence for the evening. I felt rather flattered and we went back to the Olds to introduce her, start her up and have a photo-shoot – this was the sort of thing we were all now getting used to.

Wafting from the kitchen area were some delicious aromas. Thinking that we wouldn't now have to travel into town for our meal I was looking forward to sampling the local delights. Disappointingly, we were informed that the cooking was preparation for a conference the following day.

So after checking over the Olds we headed into town, but the only café we could find was Mexican. We had nothing against Mexican food, but since we'd started out five days earlier we'd not been able to find a restaurant that served anything else.

92 miles.

DAY 6

Thursday 18th April
Globe to Show Low, Arizona

Chatting to other hotel guests before breakfast on day 6, I heard that there had been a few inches of snow the night before at Show Low, our next destination. That wasn't hard to believe, for as I made my way across the outside courtyard to the dining room the biting wind was icy.

When I'd packed back in the UK I'd assumed that the weather for most of the trip would be fairly warm, even hot, and brought clothing to suit. Fortunately, I'd included a pair of boots and thick socks, just in case. This morning I'd need them, as well as find a few other layers.

The landlady, Rebecca, told me that our journey down the Salt River Canyon would be spectacular, as it was like a smaller version of the Grand Canyon. I wasn't sure if I was excited or not and started to wonder whether the Oldsmobile – not to mention its driver – would be able to cope.

Mark, laid back as always, assured me that the Olds would have no problem.

"It couldn't be any more challenging than our first day, so stop worrying."

"OK," I replied, somewhat less confidently, "we'll see."

Heading down the steep drive from the Inn the brakes seemed to be working well and we rejoined Highway 60. From now on it was quite a climb, but I managed to get up enough speed to change into the higher gear and the Olds pulled reasonably well. Then came a plateau and as the road flattened out we increased our speed. This was high desert country and we could see an occasional ranch in the distance.

There was a strong headwind, it was icy cold and although protected by a pair of large sun-glasses, my eyes soon started to water. When the road changed direction the wind hit us from the side, buffeting the Olds about so I had to hang on tight to the tiller. This was becoming a really challenging day!

The road was in good condition, even though some of the inclines were quite steep and on a few cambered hairpin bends I needed all my strength to grip the tiller. It was difficult to judge just how strong the wind was going to be when we came to a gap, so I couldn't allow my concentration to lapse one little bit. Trying hard not to allow anything to distract my attention for more than a second or two, I managed to take the odd peek at the magnificent scenery when it felt safe to do so.

At our twenty mile service stop it was a relief to walk around in an attempt to warm up. It was surprising just how much warmer it felt without the wind blowing against us with such force. The only protection from the icy blast up on the Oldsmobile was what we were wearing, although Mark's lined windproof overalls with a hood kept him, I suspect, warmer than me.

On the roadside, there was some evidence of the previous night's snow while the mountain tops were glistening white in the sunshine.

It had been extremely cold just before leaving the UK and I was so looking forward to the USA's warmer weather. But in my wildest dreams I never imagined that we could encounter such extreme temperatures. Just two days earlier we'd been sweltering at 90°F and now it was only just above freezing and with the wind chill factor, almost unbearable.

Despite this I was enjoying the route and the incredible vista of buttes and mesas on both sides of the mountainous road, which the Olds took all in her stride. I couldn't remember the difference between a butte and a mesa until one of the locals had put me straight the previous evening at a bar in Globe.

"It's easy. A butte is a small flat-topped or pointed hill or mountain. A mesa is a medium size flat-topped hill or mountain and a plateau is a really big flat-topped hill or mountain. It was said by the early white settlers that if you could graze cattle and find water it was a mesa, not a butte."

How could I ever get confused again, it's so simple!

As we neared Salt River Canyon I noticed a sign indicating that we were at 6,200 feet. It seemed incredible that we'd climbed almost 3,000 feet above sea level in the 30 miles or so since leaving Globe, all without having to change back into low gear. We started a gradual descent along a ridge and glancing to my left, I saw a road winding down the side of the mountain. That looks a challenging drive, I thought, with no inkling that it was actually the road we were travelling on. Half a mile further on a sharp, steeply cambered left turn signalled the beginning of the descent into Salt River Canyon.

I gulped as I saw this apparently never-ending road snaking down the canyon. The strong wind didn't help my confidence. Would the brakes be efficient enough to keep the Olds at a steady speed? Will that strong wind scoop us up and send us spiralling down the mountain? That was all I could think of and I gripped the tiller as if my life depended on it – as in fact it did, and so did Mark's! What a responsibility.

As we slowly descended with other, modern cars occasionally passing us Mark suddenly pointed and said "Look over there." I glanced to my right and saw a rusty old car on the other side of the canyon, perched halfway down on the craggy rocks. It was a grisly sight – the occupants could surely not have survived.

The wind buffeted us from all sides as we changed direction on the steep curves. At one point it was hitting us head on, so strongly that braking was unnecessary. Then when we turned it battered us from the side and I had to grip the tiller hard with both hands. Over four miles and a drop of 2000 feet later we reached the bottom and the new bridge over the Salt River. The old bridge is still standing although now it looks as if it's just used as a foot-bridge.

There was a pull-in near the bottom and although a stop to regain our composure would have been desirable, the road started to climb again. The challenge of Salt River Canyon was only half completed so we decided to push on.

The ascent began again and I just managed to gain enough speed to change up into high gear. For a while the Olds kept to a steady 14 mph but as we cornered, the speed fell off and low gear reduced this to 9 mph. Fortunately there was a shoulder wide enough for the Olds, so other traffic could overtake. We could see the River Salt below in the canyon and further on, the road we had just descended, cutting into the vertical cliffs. Another five miles and we'd reached the top of the canyon. I must admit I felt a sense of relief and couldn't help but feel proud of this century old vehicle that was being worked so hard without even missing a beat.

I later discovered that back in the 1800s, the River Salt Canyon was used by Apache warriors as a refuge from pursuing US cavalry troops. It's not hard to imagine that its vertical cliffs and dramatic terrain provided a safe haven for those indigenous people. Nowadays, the river provides a border between the San Carlos Apache Reservation to the south and to the north, the White Mountain Apaches.

Once we'd reached 6,000 feet the terrain flattened and we enjoyed a trip through a ponderosa pine forest. Busy admiring this lush forest area I suddenly realised that Mark had not said a word for some time, which was unusual. I was beginning to wonder if I'd upset him in some way then suddenly there was a movement followed by a few unintelligible noises and he confessed to dozing off. I couldn't believe that anyone could possibly fall asleep seated high up in the Oldsmobile in the face of such a strong, cold wind. Oh well, there's a first time for everything!

Soon we were entering Show Low and easily found our motel.

Thinking about the day's drive, I concluded that if I'd reconnoitred the route I would have cut out the Salt River Canyon in the belief that it would be too challenging for the Oldsmobile. How wrong I'd have been! Not only had she managed every challenge she'd been put through so far, but we'd have been deprived of an incredible day's drive.

Mark and Nick started to carry out the usual checks but as soon as the sun had sunk low in the sky the temperature began to plummet and we escaped to the nearest restaurant.

Oh dear – yet another Mexican meal! At least this time the menu was a bit more extensive. And we learnt how the town came to be called Show Low.

It began as a ranch, claimed by Marion Clark and Corydon Cooley. The area, surrounded by a virgin ponderosa pine forest, had water from a creek providing irrigation, while cattle were able to graze on the lush grass.

Then Corydon Cooley became very involved with Fort Apache and began to spend considerable time there. His partner, Marion Clark, became discontented and they decided on a parting of the ways, agreeing that a game of cards should decide which one was to move. According to the tale, Clark said, "If you can show low, you win." "Show low it is," replied Cooley, turning up the two of clubs. The stakes were a 100,000 acre ranch, where the town is now located. The main street, right where our motel for the night is situated, is named 'Deuce of Clubs' in commemoration.

88 miles.

DAY 7

Friday 19th April
Show Low to St. Johns, Arizona

Emerging from my motel room I found Nick and Mark busy warming up the Oldsmobile. They told me they'd found icicles in the trailer when they'd opened it up that morning. The temperature had plummeted to minus 7° Celsius overnight – that's an incredible 20.6° Fahrenheit! No wonder I'd had to find some warm clothes during the night!

I had to search for the room where one could find breakfast. At bottom of the range motels the breakfast supplied is not what one would call 'cordon bleu'. There's usually bread of the tasteless variety, a toaster supplied to cook your own, some cereal and a mix to make waffles. So far on the trip, it's been hard to determine whether what I've been drinking was tea or coffee! On this cold morning I really needed a hot drink to prepare me for the day's driving and managed to finish a whole cupful of coffee – or was it tea?

We headed off through the wide streets of Show Low and continued on US 60 for about ten miles, turning left on to US 61. Compared to yesterday's terrain this was flat and undramatic. The road was smooth; not very wide, but that was unimportant as there was little traffic. As we progressed over the plateau, still well over 6,000 feet above sea-level, we could see the mountains in the distance. It was hard to believe we were that high up as the ground was so flat.

We passed smallholdings with a lot of farm junk lying about, giving the impression that life around here must be hard. The grass looked dry, but after another fifteen miles we arrived at Lake Concho, an eighty-acre reservoir fed by a nearby spring and used for irrigation. In recent years, it seems, the locals have been attempting to attract tourists. On the edge of the lake there are now camping facilities and the lake is stocked annually with rainbow trout.

We stopped in Concho, a small town which, in the 1800s, was built up by New Mexican sheep herders of Basque descent. In the early part of the 1900s, Mormon pioneer families came to settle at the nearby Concho Springs and the two diverse cultures blended into a unique and peaceful community concentrating on livestock farming. Like many farming communities and service towns, much of the population moved away to seek a living elsewhere during hard times such as drought, and we noticed a number of deserted properties and spaces where houses had once stood. Judging by the sign-posts at the roadside there seems to be an on-going attempt to attract retired people to the area, with inexpensive blocks of land on offer.

The road continued fairly straight with just a few rises, which the Oldsmobile dealt with easily in high gear, and in a short time we arrived on the outskirts of St Johns to see a massive complex housing the Church of Jesus Christ of Latter-day Saints.

'Town of Friendly Neighbors' read the sign as we approached. It appeared to be a peaceful place with hardly anyone about even though it was just after 1.00pm on Friday, when you'd expect people to be out shopping ready for the weekend. We were to learn that while the town may be friendly and peaceful now, it belies its early nineteenth century history when violence and murder were rife. According to the story, over a period of thirty years a battle for economic and political control of the community raged between the Mormons, the ranch owners and the Hispanic community. Within each faction there was dissent as political and family lines were crossed.

I would have liked to explore the history of the area further, but had to again remind myself that the objective of this trip was to drive a 1904 Oldsmobile from coast to coast. This left little time for such diversions, but at least we could get a smattering of information about the areas we passed through.

Our Motel was easy to find as it was in the main street, but we were so early that the rooms were not prepared, so Mark and Nick set about their daily check over the Oldsmobile. This exercise always attracts curiosity and usually disbelief that we're actually driving our 109-year-old horseless carriage on the road.

Late afternoon, I wandered up the road on my mobility scooter. There was still no traffic about – not what you'd expect at the end of the work day, even in a town of just 3,500 people. I searched for a restaurant for the evening's meal but in this town they seemed to be in short supply. Back at the motel, the cleaning lady mentioned that there was one just up a nearby side street. It was Mexican...

After yet another dose of Mexican cookery, a visit to a bar on the way back to the motel was a must. But the few locals propping up the bar awaiting their drinks gave the impression they'd been there for some time, so we soon left. I decided on an early night while the others found another bar to sample the local brew.

It had been such a short driving day that I almost felt as though I'd been skiving, but we couldn't have gone further as there were no other towns with accommodation within that day's range.

45 miles.

Time for reflection and refreshments.

Relief after exiting the tunnel before 'Top of the World'.

Am I on the right road?

Will I need to change down for this steep climb?

No sign of the Lone Ranger!

Talking to David, landlord of Leandro's bar in St. John's, Arizona.

Arriving in New Mexico.

Nick and Joy enjoying the panorama.

Spectacular rocky mesas.

The wheel spokes take a dunking to swell the wood.

The iconic Route 66 - now a quiet byway.

A Motel no more on Highway 66.

Typically rocky scenery in New Mexico.

This must be Texas!

The auto supply shop at Fort Sumner where Nick and Mark carried out the temporary valve spring repair.

The Texas police are on hand at Lubbock.

It could almost be real!

Vehicle graveyard in Texas, with an MGB still attached to a tow truck.

Straight out of a cowboy film!

Water at last - Runaway Bay, Texas.

Our friend Pete Pohlman experiences his first run in a veteran.

Teatime! Nick and Mark catch up with Stuart Barnes from the UK.

DAY 8

Saturday 20th April
St. Johns to Zuni Pueblo, New Mexico

There was no hurry to leave early, for another short day was planned before arrival at Zuni Pueblo, an Indian reservation just 56 miles away.

This time it was much warmer in the sheltered motel courtyard, but I knew that once we got going in the Olds, open to the elements, things would be different so warm clothes were again the order of the day. Although it hadn't been too warm for the past few days, we still needed to protect our skin from the bright sunlight by slapping sun-cream on our faces and the backs of hands. I'd been doing this twice a day since leaving Oceanside but my 30 factor was still too low – my face was burnt and beginning to peel and my lips were even worse, cracked and peeling with sores. What a sorry sight! Next time we drive through a big town, I thought, the highest sun factor cream will be top of my shopping list.

While I'd had an early night, David had visited the nearby Jaramillo Tavern and arranged to meet the landlord for a photoshoot with the Olds outside, before we made our way out of town.

I stopped in front of this relatively small Tavern, which looked Mexican in style with a white hacienda type facia. The landlord appeared and after the usual 'Holy Moly, you're driving that to Daytona?' he told us that his wife's ancestors had started the bar three generations back and it was the first place in Arizona to be granted a licence to sell alcohol. The present building had been opened in 1938 and the original bar, 250 yards away, was then a thriving business. But once a

Catholic church and school had been built opposite, the bar had to relocate. According to Arizona law, alcohol could not be sold within 250 yards of such buildings.

Once we were rolling along Highway 61 the cold weather conditions seemed to suit the Oldsmobile and she was chuff-chuffing along with a nice healthy sound and feel. When the mudguards start to vibrate more than usual, that's a signal to me to think about reducing the pressure on the throttle. Once up to 27mph or more the rattling becomes worse and that's the signal to drop back to a more comfortable 25.

With not a single bend for mile after mile, the road continued straight as a die, with hardly any traffic and not much interesting scenery either, just desolate, grey sandy soil with occasional tufts of grass and very little sign of human habitation. Now and again the road climbed over hills, although they weren't steep enough for the Olds to lose speed.

Just under forty miles after leaving St Johns we turned right onto Highway 53 and headed east towards Zuni. Road conditions now deteriorated dramatically. It was difficult to avoid the pot-holes and the Olds took quite a pounding. I felt annoyed that the local authority seemed to be avoiding maintaining the road that led to an Indian reservation and wondered what was in store for us after we'd crossed over the state border into New Mexico. Probably the road would be even worse.

A quick service stop and check over by Nick and Mark found that nothing, fortunately, had come adrift from the Olds and we continued. We saw picturesque mesas in the distance and more shrub-like vegetation, then I finally saw the official state sign: 'Welcome to New Mexico, the Land of Enchantment". This large, sheet metal sign was clearly a popular target for shooting practice – it was riddled with bullet holes!

The road was still straight but immediately over the State border the colour of the bitumen changed from grey to almost white. More importantly, the surface was as smooth as a billiard table. The Oldsmobile was now in her element, cresting the occasional rise with ease and any misgivings on my part were once again unfounded.

I became quite emotional when we emerged over a crest to view the most incredible panorama of multi-layered mountains and mesas in the distance. I felt sad that Trevor was not with me – he would have really enjoyed this magnificent sight.

In about fifteen miles, a sign told us we were now entering Zuni. The houses were small and made of stone, adobe or concrete blocks. I noticed outside ovens at the rear of many of them and learned later that the Zuni still bake their bread in these traditional ovens.

A sudden call of "turn right!" from Jim, my navigator for the day, and I just managed to brake in time to turn into a side street. I saw the 'Halona Plaza' in front, which looked familiar from the pictures I'd seen on the internet. As far as I could remember the guest house was just behind.

"That's it," I said to Jim.

"No, according to the GPS it's another five miles."

"Are you sure?"

I'd noticed that over the past week, Jim had an unswerving belief in the GPS, no matter what.

"Keep driving," he insisted, so I reluctantly complied.

The small houses were spread out, each on its own large block of land, until we left the community when the area ahead looked desolate. I'd started to become concerned because the wind was whipping up a gale, I'd not seen Mark and Nick in the support car for some time. It was unlike them not to be stationed at a turn-off point and I didn't trust where the GPS was taking us.

After a couple of miles I decided to stop.

"I'm going back to the town," I announced. "Then I'll ask where the guest house is."

I'm not sure if my decision was popular, but nevertheless we headed back and I pulled up in front of the Halona Plaza and hailed some locals..

"Are you looking for somewhere?" they asked.

"Yes, a guest house. Is there one here?"

"Yes, it's just round the back."

I felt relieved and took the Olds round and parked her. In a few minutes Nick and Mark arrived. They too had followed the GPS in the wrong direction but when they'd not seen us, soon turned back.

The guest house was managed by a Frenchman, who showed us to our rooms. They were a bit cramped, but at least they were warm and there was a log fire burning in the lounge.

Late in the afternoon Mark, Nick and I went for a walk and found a small museum. I was keen to find information on the area and of the Zuni people, but unfortunately it was closed. We crossed a bridge over the river and saw a lady standing at the front of her house, watching her two young sons playing. I went over and asked if she knew where I could get some local information. She told me there was a tourist information office a mile or two out of town on the main road.

I couldn't help but remark what beautiful scenery she must wake up to every morning, with those spectacular red ochre mesas overlooking the town. The mountains, she said, were sacred. They'd provided a haven for the locals to escape the Spanish Conquistadors when they entered the valley in search of gold. Apparently, the Spaniards had visited the Zuni village before and it was said that half the population lost their lives during the ensuing conflict. The next time the Zuni people became aware that the murderous Spaniards were returning they fled to the mountain. When the invaders arrived the valley flooded, drowning all their explorers and missionaries. After that, they didn't return for several hundred years..

I was asked if I'd like to see the tribal dance that was taking place just up the road. I was surprised that we, as 'foreigners', were allowed to attend. The lady's young sons said they'd show us where the dances were held and as we followed up some very rough streets, we could hear chanting and the rhythmic beat of the drums. Men were dressed elaborately in skins and feathers as they danced round in a circle. We were told that what we were seeing was part of the Corn Dance which celebrated the end of winter. When the dance finished we had to leave quickly – we'd been standing at the place where the men were traditionally about to congregate.

The Zuni, I was told, are a deeply religious tribe and nearly all social activities centre around traditional ceremonies.

Back at the guest house it was time to gather the rest of the troops and head a couple of miles out of town to get to the area's only restaurant. It was a modern building. And the food was Mexican ...

The boys were desperate for their nightly beer and were disappointed to find that no alcohol was permitted inside the reservation. So after a meal it was an early night – this time with no preliminary bar propping.

56 Miles.

DAY 9

Sunday 21st April
Zuni Pueblo to Grants, New Mexico

The morning ritual of warming up the Oldsmobile, checking the mechanicals, oiling, replenishing fuel and packing the suitcases into the trailer usually attracts a curious audience and this morning was no exception. No-one, it appeared, had ever seen such a strange looking vehicle or one that was so old and, as ever, most were amazed that we were driving the 'old girl' such a long way. Everyone wished us a safe journey and Nick and I headed off to join Highway 53 again.

Travelling east, I glanced to my right to take in the sight of those magnificent red-coloured mountains overlooking the valley. I really felt I'd like to stay here longer to explore and learn more of the history of the place, particularly of its indigenous people. Even on a casual acquaintance, the few I'd had the privilege of talking to were friendly and willing to give information about their area and culture although, I sensed, being quite cautious about it.

The road was smooth and I didn't need to be on the lookout for pot-holes, but anticipating the cold wind we both wore several layers of clothing. After about 20 miles we passed through the small farming community of Ramah. Unlike Zuni Pueblo, traditionally a Zuni community before Europeans appeared, Ramah was founded by the Mormons in the late 19th century, primarily to convert the indigenous people to their strict religion.

We spotted several signboards pointing to significant historical sites. "It's a pity we can't stop to find some of them," said Nick. I agreed, so the next time I saw a sign to what looked like an important site I turned off the road and through a pine forest. The site, it appeared, was still some miles away so we decided it would be unwise to deviate for long as the support car, still somewhere behind us, wouldn't be aware that we'd turned off. That would cause a few problems when the time came to top up with fuel and oil.

We reluctantly turned back. But as we were approaching the Highway 53 junction we saw the support car shoot past, oblivious to the fact that they'd now overtaken us. We hoped they'd eventually realise it after a few miles. A bit further along Highway 53, a car pulled alongside to say hello and take photographs and we recognised the occupants, who'd been at our guest house the night before.

"If you see our support car," yelled Nick, "can you tell them we're behind them now?" They waved and set off in pursuit of Mark and Jim.

It was an exhilarating drive. Rising and dipping, the road continued to skirt the mountains, with ponderosa pine trees on both sides as we progressed in the sunshine under a clear blue sky.

Eventually we spotted the waiting support car. They'd been stopped by our friends from the guest house, but Nick and I decided to play a bit of a game.

"Why did you pass us back there?" I asked. They were sure we must have gone off the road somewhere, but we said we'd stopped and they'd driven straight past us without noticing. They didn't believe us, but we kept up the charade for some time.

Further on was a sign telling us we were crossing the Continental Divide and that the elevation was just over 8,000 feet. No wonder it felt really cold. An extraordinary feature of the Continental Divide means that rain falling on one side of the boundary line eventually travels to one side of the continent and rain falling on the other side travels in the other direction. In other words, rain falling on opposite sides of the divide always travels to two different oceans.

It wasn't very long before we'd left the pines and the magnificent scenery behind. Although the elevation had hardly varied, the terrain flattened out and looked quite dry and barren.

Not far from Grants, our night stop, we travelled through a spread out, poor looking area in which the residents appeared to be livestock farmers. It looked really run down and so did the road, with pot-holes starting to appear again.

We were travelling along 'Ice Cave Road', which intrigued me. I later found out that when one of the old active volcanoes erupted, 10,000 years ago, it poured out about 20 miles of lava flow through a tube system over 17 miles long. Most of the lava tube collapsed, but some sections remained intact as cave structures. At one end of the collapse is a one room cave where a natural ice box has formed. The temperature in the cave never rises above 31° Fahrenheit and as rainwater and snow melt, they seep down into the cave and on to the ice deposit at the bottom, freezing new layers of ice each year.

We approached Grants over a railway line, turned right onto the main street and continued for a couple of miles beside the railway until we found our motel on the edge of the town.

While Nick and Mark checked the Olds over I went for a wander and a couple of doors down found a Chinese restaurant. I started to get excited – tonight we would have a change from Mexican!

When I returned Mark was filling up one of our large, sturdy plastic spares storage boxes with water. The spares were all over the floor and for a minute I thought he must be bonkers, but there was a logical reason for it. The boys had discovered that a spoke on one of the wooden front wheels had started to loosen, probably due to the dry atmosphere. The idea was to put the wheel into the water so that the wood would soak up the moisture and swell back to its normal state. This procedure took a couple of hours, but it was deemed successful.

Time for a shower before heading off to sample our Chinese meal and having an early night. Tomorrow would be our first 'day off'. I would be staying in Grants for the day and the rest of the team were leaving early to visit Monument Valley. I'd have liked to have seen this spectacular sight, but decided that as the key element of this trip was to arrive at Daytona Beach, still thousands of miles away, I wanted to feel fit and wide awake when we set off again the following day. I'd decided to spend the day sleeping in, washing clothes and, since my face and lips were now becoming painful with sunburn, finding somewhere that sold high factor sun-cream.

79 miles.

DAY 10

Monday 22nd April
Grants, New Mexico

I was really looking forward to my lie-in. My pattern of sleep had been topsy-turvy since I arrived in the US and I felt sleep deprived. I'd been restless every night, waking up earlier than usual and being unable to go back to sleep. Perhaps I should have gone with the others to Monument Valley after all, I thought as I heard them leaving. Oh well, what better way to spend a day off than washing and sorting out clothes and shopping – two of my least favourite activities!

To add interest to my day, I was determined to find out more about the history of the town and why it had spread along the railway line in such an elongated manner.

It was no surprise to learn that Grants had begun as a railroad camp in the 1880s when three Canadian brothers, Angus, John and Lewis Grant, were awarded a contract to build a section of the new Atlantic and Pacific Railroad through the region. Once the railway was finished, the town prospered as a result of logging in the nearby Zuni Mountains. The logs were shipped to Albuquerque where a large sawmill converted the timber to wood products.

After the decline of logging in the 1930s, Grants remained mostly as a quiet farming community until 1950, when uranium was discovered.

This site of uranium reserves turned out to be one of the largest in the world and the population of Grants boomed, from some twelve hundred people to nearly twelve thousand. Mining continued in full force until the 1982/83 recession forced the mines to close.

Situated on Route 66, which was constructed through Grants in 1937, the town survived as a tourist centre with a building boom of motels and services catering for travellers. But when in more recent times the Interstates began to be built across the US, Route 66 was decommissioned. The devastating effect this had on Grants was evident from the number of derelict motels and cafés we'd seen when we first drove along the main street.

It was time to find somewhere to shop. There was, said the receptionist, a Walmart about half a mile away. I went over and wandered around its aisles, trying to decide if a US supermarket was any different to a British one. They looked similar until, suddenly, I stopped in my tracks. Ahead was a display cabinet full of guns, from revolvers to rifles and including other nasty looking weapons. Imagine going to the local Tescos to stock up on weapons and ammunition! It was clearly commonplace here, but from my reaction it was obvious to onlookers that I was a foreigner.

I've always loathed guns. When I came to live in England I felt reassured to learn that the British 'bobby' never carried one. When I returned to Australia for a holiday seven years later, I was shocked to find that every Aussie policeman had a revolver strapped to his waist. Just before I was due to fly back to the UK I fell and injured my knee and was confined to bed for a few days. A policeman who I'd met at a party and become friendly with was in the area and he decided to visit me. He was still on duty and in uniform and I was mortified to see a revolver strapped to his body.

Despite the shock of seeing that display cabinet, it didn't take me long to find the highest factor sun-cream. I bought it and left.

I was looking forward to the rest of the team returning as I had a surprise for them. I'd discovered a steak restaurant in the hotel opposite and booked a table so we wouldn't miss out. Two nights without a Mexican meal!

I wasn't disappointed – a nice, big American steak with salad. Naturally, the conversation was all about Monument Valley and I began to wish I'd gone with them.

I also decided that I didn't like days off. I missed driving the Oldsmobile and hearing its rhythmic phut-phut-phut in my ear throughout the day.

I started to get excited about the next day, when we'd be following the iconic Route 66.

0 miles

DAY 11

Tuesday 23rd April
Grants to Albuquerque, New Mexico

It was very late, after 10.30am, when we eventually got away from Grants.   Jim had a complication with a business transaction and after countless phone-calls, it transpired that he needed to sign documents that were in the UK. This meant he had either to fly to the UK or arrange for the documents to be available in the US.

With around a hundred miles to cover to our next stop, Albuquerque, I was becoming anxious with all this hanging about. I decided it would be better to head off in the Oldsmobile with Mark and we'd meet Jim in the support car later, once he'd sorted everything out. This might not be for several hours, so Mark made sure we had fuel and oil supplies in our rear trunk. He also, somewhat reluctantly, conceded that he'd have to survive without his regular cup of tea along the route.

Route 66 ran parallel to the Interstate 40. We could see the heavy traffic thundering along as we merrily chuffed away on a traffic-free road in the sunshine. Bliss!

I was enjoying myself. The road wasn't as smooth as expected and I had to dodge the occasional pothole, but to view the red mesas set against the bright blue sky made it all worthwhile.

I felt a bit dejected as we passed derelict motels, service stations and diners overrun with weeds and creepers and with tumbleweed collecting in the driveways. Signs dangling in the breeze signified the end of a more prosperous time when Route 66, which John Steinbeck had immortalised as the 'Mother Road', was the country's lifeline, taking people and resources from Chicago through the Midwest, the Southwest and into California.

We could see from the amount of traffic on the nearby Interstate that this was the road that most of the population now used, apart from the few searching for the excitement of a bygone era. Interstate users miss out on natural scenery as the old road dips, climbs and flows among its surroundings, whereas the new road cuts through hills and continues straight ahead to meet the 21st century's demand for fast travel and delivery of goods.

After about an hour we were passed by the support car and trailer. Jim had sorted out his problem and before long Mark would be able to have his cup of tea at the next service stop.

In another 45 miles Route 66 merged with the Interstate. I'd thought it would still carry on alongside, but after we'd crossed the Interstate bridge the support team were parked up. There was a road, of sorts, but judging by its surface the maintenance team had obviously not been around since Route 66 was decommissioned in 1984!

David went down the road to check if it was suitable for the Oldsmobile.

"It's rough," he said on his return. "Full of deep pot-holes and corrugations. They look unavoidable."

"Not again," I said.

" 'Fraid so. It's worse than that rough road we were on a couple of days ago."

The alternatives were either to use the road or to trailer the Oldsmobile. The latter wasn't an option, so Mark and I pushed on at a steady walking pace, trying unsuccessfully to avoid the potholes and rocks that were strewn about. After what seemed like hours, but was a mere 10 miles, we arrived at a better surface and stopped to check the mudguard bolts. That they'd not come loose was miraculous, considering the severe vibration the Olds had been subjected to.

We now had to detour on another minor road, which would enter Albuquerque from the south instead of from the west as originally planned. This would add another 18 miles to the day's total; nearly an hour, but probably more as our average speed had dropped considerably due to that rough section.

There were still about 45 miles to go to Albuquerque, but at least the road's condition was reasonable. Then a vigorous side wind suddenly got up and the Olds began to be severely buffeted. Dust swirled about and we tried to miss the tumbleweed blowing at high speed across the road.

Fiercely gusting, the wind kept changing direction and as the road became busier, trucks passing in the opposite direction made conditions worse. It was hard to judge just how strong the next gust would be. With all this pounding, my arm started to ache from the extra pressure needed to control the tiller steering. I could see Mark's right hand poised, ready to help if needed.

Every time we went over a crest I hoped the wind would have abated on the other side. It didn't, and I started to feel this constant battering would never end. As we got closer to Albuquerque the traffic became busier and I began to worry that the Olds would blow across the road into its path. It was difficult to feel positive with such negative thoughts racing through my mind. I tried to convince myself that this trip was meant to be fun, after all it was me that had chosen to drive the Olds myself from coast to coast, it was no-one else's decision. But fun this was definitely not! No matter what I thought I still felt frightened and I was sure Mark felt the same.

Ten miles from the centre of Albuquerque and with buildings in sight, I felt sure things would improve. Surely the wind was bound to die down in a built-up area. It didn't. The buildings were spread out with empty blocks in between that seemed to be covered in grey sand. The gusts increased in intensity, scooping up sand from the blocks and surrounding hills. It felt like driving through a sand blasting machine as the coarse grains hammered our faces. We were both wearing large, curved sun-glasses but the sand was still getting into our eyes. We had to squint to protect them, which made it even more difficult to see through the swirling dust clouds.

It was near the end of the business day, the traffic was quite heavy and we stopped at so many red lights that I started to feel that we'd never arrive at the hotel. Eventually, as we drove through the Old Town part of the city, it came into view. I'd never felt so relieved as when we manoeuvred the Olds to the front of the foyer. I had to sit for a few minutes to convince myself that today's challenge was over. We'd survived it well, the Oldsmobile had never missed a beat. Once again I felt very proud of her.

After the Olds' evening check we showered to get rid of the layers of sand and dust. I was now beginning to understand why drivers and passengers in the early 1900s covered their normal clothing with 'dusters' when they drove the new horseless carriages.

Around the corner from our hotel we found a variety of restaurants to choose from and settled on an Asian noodle bar. Nick was delighted to find a 'smoke shop' that sold special cigarette lighters that would work in a strong breeze. He was eager to try it out – I wasn't!

103 miles.

DAY 12

Wednesday 24th April
Albuquerque to Vaughn, New Mexico

The temperature had barely risen above freezing point when we set off at 9.05am but the quality of our breakfast had been unusually acceptable, which set us up for braving the cold air. The sun was shining brightly and there was no wind, at least not so far, but I wasn't going to fool myself into believing that we'd seen the last of the previous day's squalls.

Our progress through the urban area was not too bad. Most people must have already been at work as there were no traffic queues – even the traffic lights were favouring us today, but then Albuquerque is a much smaller city than Phoenix, where we'd been snarled up before. The population of the 475 square miles of Phoenix is around one and a half million while in Albuquerque, at about 180 square miles, it's nearer to half a million.

It's no wonder it took over two hours to get out of Phoenix. If I were planning this trip again I'd avoid all cities. I find the smaller towns, and the reasons for their existence, much more interesting.

Once out of town we started to climb gradually through Route 66's rugged mountain road. RV parks on both sides of the road, particularly where the views were spectacular, indicated that this must be a holiday destination. We also noticed a number of small communities nestling against the mountain slopes. The Oldsmobile was pulling well, not dropping below 18 mph on the gentle inclines, and when we'd reached 7,000 feet above sea-level the road started to level out.

This was pleasant motoring, but I'd have enjoyed it even more if the air blowing into our faces had been warmer.

As the terrain levelled out and the road straightened we seemed to be entering ranch territory, with a scattering of smallholdings. After almost 40 miles we arrived at Highway 41, which would take us south. We said goodbye to the famous Route 66 and entered the town of Moriarty. Apart from a few modern shops and businesses connected with agriculture, the town looked as though it had seen better days, perhaps when Route 66 had been fully operational. There were the usual closed diners, garages and motels that we'd become used to seeing all along that historic route.

Passing a service station, I spotted Mark and Nick replenishing the jerry can with fuel for the Olds. It was almost time for our stop but I kept driving; the support team would pull into a more convenient position out on the road once they'd overtaken us. Often, they'd pick a place with a nice view but that would be hard to find in this almost featureless landscape. The mountains in the far distance were not on our route today, but I could settle for anywhere. I was so enjoying the contrasting scenery we were experiencing every day since we set out from the Pacific coast twelve days earlier. It felt like an age away, but it was less than two weeks ago.

The names of roads certainly gave clues to the local activities. Seeing Rancho Grande Road, White Ranch Road, Tree Farm Road and Ice Plant Road I came to the conclusion that this was a farming area!

It was hard to believe that we were still over 6,000 feet above sea-level. The countryside stayed flat and the grass dry, reminding me of the Australian outback – albeit with a contrasting temperature. For some reason I'd convinced myself that as soon as we started heading south, the temperature would rise significantly and I could throw off the thick clothing and waterproofs. No such luck!

For thirty miles we continued on the dead straight 41 without a single curve or corner. Then as it came to its end we turned left onto Highway 60, which ran right beside the railway line on the outskirts of the small, run-down town of Willard. With a population of only a couple of hundred, Willard had been set up by ranchers. When the railway was built it became a local shipping port for ranchers and farmers. More recently the trains had ceased to stop here and people had moved away, leaving nature to take its toll on their small houses. It certainly looked as though it had, and with a vengeance.

Just as I was beginning to believe that we'd reached the end of the contrasting scenery we were surrounded by what looked like lakes of dried salt. The road meandered up a few short inclines, then down again through the Great Salt Lake. Heading towards us, I saw that what looked from a distance like a whirlwind. It appeared to be white sand, but as we were travelling next to a salt lake it was probably mainly salt with a bit of sand mixed in. We came to a curved incline and suddenly the wind hit us head on. We were completely smothered with this white grit and the fierce blast immediately knocked 10mph off the Oldsmobile's speed.

After a few more miles, and still 40 miles from our night stop at Vaughn, the road became a dual carriageway. Big trucks belted past and once more that dreaded side-wind pelted the Olds and its occupants. I was beginning to wonder when the 'fun' part of this trip would begin.

A number of trains passed us by and I made a new discovery: If I waved to the driver he would blast his really loud klaxon, whereas if I didn't wave I would get no acknowledgement. Several trains passed us and this became something of an obsession – if I didn't get a response I felt really rejected.

We stopped for servicing about 20 miles from Vaughn, which gave us time to study the length of the trains. They seemed to go on forever. Some were as much as two miles long, completely full of shipping containers and powered by four locomotives, two at the front and two at the rear. Their lengths varied and some only had three locos, but no train was less than one mile long.

At last we arrived at Vaughn. It was obvious the town had a railway heritage as it had developed along the railway line, but as with so many of these small towns, prosperity had deserted it. We passed empty blocks where buildings once stood, boarded up houses and businesses until, at the far end of town, we arrived at our accommodation, a motel with a modern version of a traditional diner at the front. It was 5.30pm and it had been a long day, so I was looking forward to finishing my duties, having a warm shower and later on relaxing in the American diner.

The car park looked full and I drove around looking for a vacant parking space when Mark and Nick appeared.

"The place is full," they said, "and they haven't honoured our booking."

I'd been trying to school myself into not getting stressed at moments like this. You can always find an alternative. Fortunately, there was a 'mom and pop' motel at the other end of town where we'd come in, and having found that our original motel was full David had gone back and booked rooms. Then I remembered that Eni, the assistant cameraman, had been waving to us as we entered Vaughn. I'd thought it was strange that she wasn't peering through a camera viewfinder. I'd waved back to her and it never occurred to me that she was frantically gesturing. She was, of course, pointing out our revised accommodation.

The 'mom and pop' were welcoming and friendly people. The motel was a bit run down but it was clean and the rooms were more spacious than we'd previously been accustomed to.

Mark was becoming concerned that the Oldsmobile had started to run lean and discovered the inlet valve spring was softening. After some deliberation he and Nick decided to make a $1/4$ inch thick collar to put under the spring to increase its pressure. A front tyre, too, had been wearing on the edge and Mark also decided that tonight was the night to change it around. Both these maintenance jobs were time-consuming and at about 7.00pm Mark announced that he had to eat something or he'd fall over!

We noticed one of the other motel guests walking back to his room carrying a pizza. When I asked him where he'd bought it he pointed to a run-down café opposite, but said they were closing down for the day. So David and Jim drove to the only other eating establishment in the town, the American diner, to bring us back a take-away. Nick and Mark's room became the dining room for the evening and they'd just finished the maintenance and tested the Olds when our 'meals on wheels' arrived.

I learned that Vaughn is probably best known these days for its police force, which now consists of a single, drug-sniffing dog. Last year there had been a police chief, but apparently he owed tens of thousands of dollars and was accused of selling one of the town's rifles and keeping the proceeds. A second officer had recently pleaded guilty to assault and battery. When time allows, the County Sheriff's Department now patrols Vaughn. It's reputed to be a stopover for drug smugglers, which must at least keep the dog busy.

127 miles.

DAY 13

Thursday 25th April
Vaughn to Clovis, New Mexico

It was so cold when I poked my head out of the door first thing in the morning that I had to find another layer of clothing before walking over to have breakfast in reception. It was the usual tea, or was it coffee – I still couldn't tell the difference – and a packet of small doughnuts. If they tasted of anything it was equally uninteresting, but at least they would build up the sugar levels before setting out on yet another extremely cold day.

Nick was my passenger for the day. Well wrapped up in Mark's padded overalls, gloves and mittens he said he wished he'd brought his warm boots, which were back in the UK. He never guessed that we'd experience such freezing weather.

We left on time at 9.00am. Nick was anxious to get rolling so he could try out his new 'breeze free' cigarette lighter. Before long it was time to roll a cigarette and test it. The lighter proved a roaring success – but in the stiff breeze the cigarette burnt through all too quickly for the smoker...

The straight road stretched for miles into the distance, rising and falling over the High Plain that was still over 6,500 feet above sea-level. The terrain seemed to be even more featureless than the day before – no mountains or trees, just the occasional small tufts of grass. We guessed it was ranch country but only saw the occasional small building, some abandoned in a state of complete disrepair. I could imagine how traumatic it must have been for the former residents with no alternative but to vacate their houses and land without financial compensation.

After ten miles we stopped to check the oil level. It was so cold I had to walk around to get all my joints moving, I was stiff and could hardly move. It didn't help when Mark and Jim said how hot it was in the support car with the heating full on. I made a mental note to remember that – one day I'll have my revenge!

58 miles after leaving Vaughn we arrived at Fort Sumner. Nick and Mark had decided that we needed to find a motor factor to buy some hardened shims, as the collar they'd made the night before for the valve spring was just temporary. We'd already telephoned Gary Hoonsbeen, who had some springs in stock and promised to send them to the motel we'd booked in Graham, a few nights further on. He'd spoken to Daisy, the motel manager, who'd promised to personally look out for the parcel.

We saw Mark and Jim in the support car parked in the street, directly in front of a motor factors shop that also sold fishing tackle. We stopped there for some time while Mark and Nick fitted the new shims on the spot.

This provided an opportunity to talk to the locals, from whom I learnt that Fort Sumner had gained its name in 1863 when it was built to incarcerate the Apache population. It was closed five years later and the fort was sold to a prominent New Mexico landowner. But everyone I spoke to told me that Fort Sumner is better known as the place where the murderous outlaw Billy the Kid was shot in 1881. He was buried locally, but in 1904 the Pecos River flooded the cemetery and all the markers and even some remains of the dead were washed away. As late as 1932, money was raised to purchase a headstone, but nobody really knew where his grave was. The exact location still seems in doubt. We passed a sign saying 'See Billy the Kid's real grave', only to find another one further on which read 'Billy the Kid Museum'. Both signs were different and totally independent.

With the adjustments to the Olds completed we carried on. At our next 25 mile stop the weather seemed a little warmer, although I couldn't yet dispose of the layers of clothing. The Olds was running well and Mark thought that after the repair the exhaust note was sounding much healthier – no more hiccups or backfiring on the overrun due to that soft valve spring.

A few miles from Clovis we found more functional farms. Clovis, like all the towns we'd recently passed through, has a railway heritage stemming from when the Santa Fe Railroad began its first transcontinental route through this area of open prairie land in 1907. Unlike the others, which have become almost ghost towns, Clovis appeared to be thriving

We entered the outskirts on a dual carriageway and at 5.15pm found our Day's Inn Motel without any difficulty. We also noticed a few cafés nearby, so at least we'd have a choice this evening.

Clovis has significant agricultural and ranching activities, including peanut and cotton farming and cattle ranching used for both meat and dairy produce. Several processing plants exist for these products, which provide employment for thousands of people. Another source of economic stability for the city is the Cannon Air Force Base, housing almost 3,000 service personnel. But as we live in an ever changing world, I could imagine the devastating effect on the city if one of these large enterprises closed.

After the driving day had finished, Mark checked the valves again and was satisfied the way the engine was running. With many miles still to go before the end of our epic trip, I hoped that the Oldsmobile would be able to survive without any other problems.

120 miles

DAY 14

Friday 26th April
Clovis to Lubbock, Texas

It was an easy run out of Clovis, an extra wide road and not too much traffic.

Still dressed in winter woollies, it wasn't long before I starting shedding the layers at last. The weather was definitely warmer. It's extraordinary to think that after several days of freezing, today, suddenly, we were warm.

After ten miles we'd left New Mexico and entered Texas, the fourth State on this trip. I always get excited when we cross a State line and usually cheer, as it feels like we've achieved something. The roads were straight, running parallel to the railway and the land was flat as we passed through cattle country. There appeared to be more agricultural activity than in New Mexico. with grain elevators and silos in the small towns. Some of the land had been ploughed ready for planting spring crops.

Long freight trains were still passing us in both directions and as usual I waved, seeking acknowledgement from the train driver. Today it was working well – everyone blew their hooters!

I've said before that when seated in the Olds, exposed to the elements and not in a box like a modern car, you can smell the pleasant aromas of plants and flowers. But it sure wasn't pleasant today, driving close to the cattle farms – oh for the wonderful scent of orange blossom that we'd experienced on our first day in California! As we'd found before with cattle, the Olds caused havoc with the ones in Texas, which seemed set to stampede whenever we got close to them. I couldn't quite understand this as the exhaust note is not loud. It must be due to the slow beat of the 2-litre, single cylinder 'one bang every lamp-post' engine. Perhaps the cows were more in tune with V8s.

The Olds chugged along as usual without missing a beat. As ever, she created enormous interest with people waving from their cars and taking photographs. We'd now been on the road for two weeks and had become used to the dramatic scenery with the Olds managing some extremely tough conditions, but it was still necessary to maintain 100% concentration. I have to admit that when driving on the flat all day I have to keep my imagination active. I started to think about bygone days in this area when bison used to roam freely. There were an estimated 20 to 30 million bison roaming North America, before unregulated shooting during the 1870s reduced the population to about a thousand in about 20 years. Today, approximately 500,000 bison live across North America. Most are not pure bison but have been cross-bred with cattle and raised as livestock on ranches. Fewer than 30,000 bison are in conservation herds. I'd never seen a bison and it didn't look as if I'd have the opportunity on this trip.

Mark was alongside me on the Olds today. Typically, he noticed that a passing truck had yellow flashing lights instead of the usual red. Clearly, the scenery wasn't interesting enough to keep him occupied!

The further east we travelled, the bigger the towns started to become. We passed through Muleshoe, spread out and still with some abandoned buildings, but obviously involved mostly with farm supply manufacturing and feed processing plants, as well as its dairy industry.

Littlefield was even bigger and with its own bypass, which we used. We'd noticed signs at many of the towns we passed through claiming some kind of world or State record for the biggest or best artefact. Littlefield's claim to fame is to have had the world's tallest windmill. Built in the early 1900s, it stood until 1926 when the 132 foot high structure was blown over. A replica was built, but it only stands at a mere 112 feet. Littlefield economy is diverse but it traditionally depends on cotton, this part of Texas being a significant cotton growing area.

It still felt as if I'd not driven my quota of miles when we reached the outskirts of our destination, Lubbock. Driving on the flat without rises, dips or even mountains to negotiate we'd made excellent progress, arriving at 4.30 Texas time. To us though, having started the day from Clovis, it was only 3.30 New Mexico time.

Lubbock was clearly a bigger city than we'd seen for some while, a sign indicating a population of 218,000. It has a thriving farming industry with cotton the main source of income. The area went from producing four bales of it in 1902 to producing over 100,000 in 1932. Today, Lubbock County produces an astonishing two to three million bales of cotton per year.

One of Lubbock's claims to fame is that it's the birthplace of Buddy Holly, the singer/song-writer tragically killed in an aeroplane accident when he was just 22 years old. To this day, I remember from my youth his song 'Peggy Sue'.

The motel we'd booked on the outskirts of Lubbock was on the Interstate frontage road but the GPS didn't want to take us on minor roads. It was leading us to Interstate 27 which we needed to avoid. We escaped down a side street before we inadvertently ended up on the big road without any way of getting off it. There were potholes galore and I was having difficulty avoiding them. I wondered why, in such an apparently thriving community, the local council hadn't maintained the road.

Sitting waiting for a red traffic light to change, Mark spotted a sheriff's car was behind us.

"I'm going to stop him and ask directions," he declared, gesturing to the sheriff to follow us. I pulled up in a sort of car park where a building had once stood and he pulled up alongside. He didn't get out of his car, so Mark asked for directions through the side window. Still sitting in the car, the sheriff asked if he could take a photo of the Olds. We had to wait until he'd finished a long phone call before he finally poked his camera out of the window and took the shot. We thought it strange that he didn't get out of the car, then decided it might be standard policy; who knows, we might have a weapon or even be terrorists – with our fast get-away car!

After a few miles and more red lights, which I was careful not to run as our sheriff friend was still following, we arrived at our destination. He'd stayed with us until we arrived, then blew his horn and waved as he sped off.

Mark had been pleased with the performance of the Oldsmobile, but a spark plug check showed she was running rich because of the lower altitude. A small adjustment fixed it and as it was still early and warm we all went for a swim. I needed the exercise after sitting in the Oldsmobile all day for the past two weeks.

There was nowhere to eat nearby, so it meant a trip for a few miles in the support car to an American steak house, which we were all looking forward to. When we arrived there was a long queue stretching out to the door. We thought we'd be waiting for hours until they'd all eaten, then discovered that you had to queue to order, then pay, then you'd be shown to a table. Seemed a strange system and a bit awkward for us as, unlike the locals, we didn't know what was on the menu. But we managed OK and experienced our first Texas steak. It was certainly worth queuing for.

120 miles.

DAY 15

Saturday 27th April
Lubbock to Aspermont, Texas

Jim and I headed off from the motel, immediately crossed over Interstate 27, turned left and in another 100 yards turned right and we were on Highway 84, a dual carriageway heading south-east. There was no urban traffic and just one traffic light to contend with this morning then we were in open countryside with only a few agricultural supply businesses beside the road.

This was good, as I was starting to dislike driving the Olds in heavy traffic and hoped the cities further on were not going to be too big. But just as I was enjoying this quiet road I heard a sudden screech of tyres to my right. I looked across saw a car passing me on the shoulder, completely out of control and facing the wrong way. I braked, the car slewed in front of the Olds, headed for the armco barrier separating the carriageways, then spun back in front of us and stopped on the shoulder, facing in the right direction.

It was a bizarre and frightening incident. The driver was young with a young lady beside him. I didn't stop, but kept rolling on feeling nervous and realising just how vulnerable we were in the Oldsmobile. We guessed the young driver had been speeding and not concentrating, suddenly becoming aware of us on the road in front of him. It was a good job he did finally realise we were there otherwise I probably wouldn't be here to tell the tale.

A few miles up the road Nick and Mark were waiting for a debriefing session. They were aware of our near miss as David, who had by now caught up with them, had pulled into a service station where an employee had witnessed the whole episode.

We carried on but I had difficulty in erasing the incident from my mind. I tried to concentrate on the scenery, which was flat countryside without much vegetation, but the red ochre fields had been ploughed ready for cotton to be planted. A number of 'nodding donkeys' were doing their work drilling for oil, the smell of crude oil being quite strong as we drove along. For mile after mile the scenery remained unchanged; a never-ending succession, it seemed, of ploughed paddocks and oil pumps.

It was a pity we wouldn't have the opportunity of seeing the cotton plants growing. The soil temperature needs to be a minimum of 60°F for ten days before the seeds can be planted and the air temperature had been unseasonably cold, a fact of which we were well aware on this trip,.

Just before we arrived at the small town of Post, we climbed a rise and there in front of us was green grass and a few trees. Post looked quaint, its main street lined with gift and clothing stores based in restored, historic buildings. It reminded me of a refurbished wild-west town, but without the gun-slingers.

Turning left on to Highway 380, we headed west towards our day's destination in Aspermont and, amazingly, started to climb again. The road had little traffic, was well maintained, there was green vegetation and it felt like we were in a different state. But we were still in Texas and this part of it was certainly not flat and uninteresting.

After some miles of climbing – which the faithful Olds took in its stride – I could see mountains in the distance and up ahead a custom built shelter and picnic area for tourists. This one, however, looked unusual – it had both a Union Jack and a Stars and Stripes flying on the roof. The rest of the team had arrived, set up lunch and put up the flags that we'd used on the Oldsmobile at the Oceanside start. They'd even put out the strip of carpet used when any of them needed to lie under the Oldsmobile to check its mechanicals. How upmarket our lunch venue was today, complete with a table and seats! So different to other days, when we had to eat our sandwiches standing up.

The road continued to be quiet and in good condition. We passed through the outskirts of Jayton, a small farming service town judging by the number of agricultural machinery vendors. Further on there was a business selling 'cowboy crafts', indicating that this was cowboy and ranch country.

I'm not quite sure what I'd been expecting when we arrived at Aspermont for our night's stay. The translation of the town's name is 'rough mountain' and I'd conjured up the idea of a pleasant town, situated on a small mountain with picturesque old colonial houses surrounded by greenery and exotic plants. As usual, I was way out!

Aspermont was a typical farm town, spread out, dusty, with no green grass and numerous boarded-up buildings and empty blocks. The motel we were booked into was easy to find. It was just on the outskirts and next door was the only restaurant in town. It catered mainly for truck drivers but at least the temperature was in the region of 82° Fahrenheit. Wonderful!

While Nick and Mark were checking the Olds over after the day's 116 mile run, the routine, as ever, attracted passers by. One chap, Eddie, was captivated by the Oldsmobile and idea of our trip. But I arrived to find the rest of the team were looking unusually forlorn. I wondered what the problem was, and being a bit of a pessimist I started to think that there was something wrong with my ancient vehicle. But no. The problem was that they'd been informed by Eddie that Aspermont is a dry town, meaning that alcohol is not available and is forbidden to be sold. So no beer tonight and no bar for the boys to prop up until the wee hours. But Eddie had a solution. There was a liquor store 14 miles out of town. He offered to drive one of the team members out there to purchase 'illegal' supplies.

As Mark and Nick were still fettling the Oldsmobile, Eddie roared off in his Utility with Jim, the familiar deep throbbing of the V8 engine disappearing into the distance. When they arrived back Jim was embarrassed – Eddie had paid for the liquor and under no circumstances would he accept any reimbursement, although he did have a beer with the boys. An excellent example of American hospitality! We were also told that (whisper it) we could take the bottles into the restaurant next door, where the staff would hide the booze behind the counter and bring it to the table when required.

Whilst each engaged in demolishing a hamburger we were joined by another motel guest, a truck driver. During the conversation he happened to mention that we should really be displaying a triangle on the back of the Olds, denoting a slow vehicle. Apparently it's the law in this State. We decided that as soon as we arrived in a big town we would acquire one, in case the sheriffs in Texas were not as friendly as the ones who'd previously been waving to us nearly every day.

116 miles

DAY 16

Sunday 28th April
Aspermont to Graham, Texas

Most unusually, Nick and I set out on time this morning at 9.00am. The motel didn't provide breakfast so while the rest of the team went off to the café next door for bacon and eggs we got going on the hundred-odd mile drive to Graham.

It was Sunday and Aspermont was quiet as we passed through. Perhaps people were getting ready for church. Indeed we'd noticed a number of large, very modern churches. Even with a population of less than a thousand, this small town has four really big ones. Unlike the UK of today, here religion plays a major part in everyday life.

This, we thought, should be an easy day. All we had to do was continue straight to Graham on Highway 380 with no need to look for any other turn-off. I was only the driver, so I took instructions from my navigator for the day who is always in possession of our hand-held GPS system, set up by Jim every evening in readiness for the following day's journey.

Once through the town the terrain was similar to the previous day, with vast areas of ploughed fields waiting for seeds to be planted. Further on were uncultivated areas with stunted trees. The gently undulating highway was well maintained and I was starting to enjoy my day. I did notice a sign on our highway indicating 'south', but it was no cause for panic. I was confident the highway would start veering to the left at some point, so we'd be heading east.

Seven miles later, Nick declared that the GPS didn't seem to be working correctly. It was trying to get us to turn round and the indicated mileage to our destination, instead of decreasing, was increasing. After another mile or so we both realised we were heading south, not east. Yes, we were on the wrong road! I should have realised that the sun was not shining in my eyes, as it usually does every morning when we head east. We turned around and headed back. This was always going to be a long day and now it would be even longer.

I thought it might be a good idea to phone the other members of the team as they'd be driving relatively quickly to catch us up, thinking we'd be ahead of them. Knowing my luck, I expected to find no mobile phone service this far out in the sticks. But my luck was in. I got through just as they were leaving the café and about to set off. Nick was more than happy that I'd made the call – he now had time for another cigarette!

Fifty minutes later we arrived back where we'd started from, to be informed by the team that their bacon, egg, sausage and coffee had been excellent. I felt envious. It transpired that instead of turning left down the 380 on the outskirts of town, we'd headed straight on along Highway 83. Neither Nick nor I had spotted the sign!

The terrain seemed to change as we finally headed east and the roads stretched on for miles without any turns. Once again the driver felt she was having an easy day as we rumbled past cattle ranches and farms with massive irrigation systems, all on well maintained roads. The further east we went, the greener the terrain became; even the road-side verges, which suggested a recent rainfall. I was glad it hadn't been today! Our cameraman David Winstanley had been keen for us to experience heavy rainfall just to give him a bit of variety for his film. Enjoying the sunshine and wearing just one layer of clothing, I wasn't quite so keen.

About 20 miles out of Aspermont (although, because of our 'wrong slot', more like 36 miles for us) we could see ahead the small town of Rule. The farming towns in Texas reminded me of similar towns in Australia, particularly the

Wimmera a large wheat-growing area in the west of Victoria where my father came from. The streets are wide, the architecture is similar and the towns are spread out. There were clumps of trees on empty blocks and brick chimneys where once stood wooden houses. They would most likely have been either split up and transported to other areas or demolished altogether. When I was a child we occasionally used to visit Minyip, Victoria, where my father was brought up. It was nothing unusual to see two trucks in convoy, each transporting half a house.

As we drove through the middle of Rule, sturdy two-storey brick buildings with surrounding verandahs, where banks, post offices and saloons once traded, displayed the same early 1900s design used in colonial outposts everywhere. In the main street, a local artist had decorated one long, dilapidated brick building with a large mural depicting a street scene of 1908. I was surprised at the big, modern churches in the town, all with overflowing car parks. It gave the impression that religion here was thriving. It was clear as we drove through it that the town's economy was mainly involved with wheat, peanuts and cotton.

During one of our service stops we were joined by a motorcyclist, not on a Harley but riding, somewhat unusually, a Kawasaki. He was yet another to be amazed that we were actually driving such an old 'contraption' on the road. The boys were most interested to learn from him a key piece of information – which areas where dry and which sold alcohol.

With the road still straight and in excellent condition, we were passed and re-passed by our motorcycling friend. The land was flat, a lack of roadside fences and the occasional crop growing in its early stages giving us an impression of vast space extending for miles.

We passed through two more small towns of similar layout to Rule until, some twelve miles from our day's destination, the road turned left and we entered Newcastle. Early in the last century, coal had been found in the area and the town was named after Newcastle-upon-Tyne, then the UK's major coal producing city. But housing just 600 people this Texas town was much smaller and coal production had ceased back in 1942.

We were almost through the town when the road turned sharp right. At last I was getting practice with the tiller steering again having hardly deviated from the straight and narrow all day. As I was turning past what looked like a park, we could hear hymns being sung and noticed crowds of people attending an outdoor religious service. I almost felt like a heathen for not attending a church service somewhere, considering that on this Sabbath day most of the population appeared to be engaged in worshipping.

The support car was parked just by the park. I couldn't believe that the rest of the team were attending the church service, but it turned out that the motorcyclist had told them there was a shop nearby that sold alcohol and Jim had gone to stock up.

Near Graham there were trees with green leaves, the first we'd seen for some time, and a couple of lakes which appeared to offer boating facilities. It looked as if we'd left the desert and the isolation behind us.

Graham has a population of less than 10,000 and although our motel was on the other side of town it didn't take long to find it. Mark and Jim were already there when we arrived and Daisy, the motel manager, had handed over to Mark the parcel of long-awaited valve springs that Gary had posted from Minneapolis. I'm not sure what Gary had told Daisy during their telephone conversation, but she enthused about our trip and even gave us one room free.

I'd thoroughly enjoyed every second of my day – and the big surprise was that we'd arrived in Graham at 3.45pm. I could probably have driven another 40 miles or so!

Mark was keen to fit the new inlet valve spring and our early arrival meant that he had time to finish the job before sunset. Then it was off to find a restaurant that was open. Tonight would be Italian food, so I got to practise a little of the now very rusty Italian that I'd studied at university in Perugia in my early twenties just, er, a few years ago..

123 miles.

DAY 17

Monday 29th April
Graham to Denton, Texas

While Nick and Jim went off to find somewhere to buy that warning triangle that we'd been told in Aspermont we should have, Mark and I headed up the road in the Oldsmobile. There was quite a lot of traffic and I was anxious to get out on the open road again. After a couple of miles the GPS started bleeping like it usually does when it thinks we've gone wrong.

"What's wrong with that thing?" I asked.

"It thinks we're going in the wrong direction." I stopped on the side of the road while Mark checked the GPS map.

"We'll have to turn round," he said.

"What? Not again!" I retorted, throwing in the odd expletive or two.

Back through the traffic we went, turning right on to Highway 380 after a few miles. We noticed the support car and trailer parked outside an industrial unit and guessed that the lads had found somewhere to buy a triangle.

The roads were wide with, at first, not much traffic. I was certainly enjoying myself going up the rises and down again, the Olds behaving magnificently as we motored through agricultural land. The trees and the dams that were apparently full suggested that here in Texas, more rain falls than in New Mexico that we'd left behind us. We passed through several farm towns with the usual empty blocks or boarded-up buildings as well as some businesses looking as if trade was brisk.

About 50 miles out from Graham we came to Runaway Bay. This appealed to me as it looked the perfect place to actually run away to. Alongside was a man-made expanse of water called Lake Bridgeport, originally built as a reservoir in 1929 to prevent the Trinity River from flooding. Now it's also used as a recreational area offering boating, fishing and plots of land on which to build holiday homes. Crossing the mile-long bridge over the lake felt wonderful. We'd not seen such a stretch of water since we left the coast more than a couple of weeks back. The sun was shining, the air was pleasant and I was wearing just short sleeves and no hat, with the breeze blowing through my hair. At last we were experiencing beautiful warm weather and it had been such a pleasure this morning to finally pack away all the winter clothing, the thick socks, gloves and boots.

We passed through verdant forests and beside the road, for mile after mile, grew wild flowers of every colour and hue. From dry, almost desert-like terrain to today's lush greenery, the State of Texas was offering us considerable variety in just three days.

At our service stop, Nick brought out the warning triangle they'd bought in Graham. Using a temporary fastening of cut down inner-tube, it was fixed to the back of the seat where it would be most visible.

Near Decatur, a city of 6,000 plus people, and still with over thirty miles to go, the road became much busier. Columns of big trucks overtook us on the dual carriageway ring road, keeping Mark busy as he continually turned around to keep an eye on the traffic behind us. When a big truck was coming he would warn me and I'd pull over as much as I could. We came to quite a steep hill and the Olds dropped back to about 15 miles an hour, so we were soon engulfed by enormous, laden trucks. As I neared the top of the hill Mark suggested I'd better pull up on the shoulder as right behind us was a car with flashing lights. It was the local sheriff. Oh dear, what now, I thought.

The sheriff walked up to the back of the car and Mark hopped out. He was asked for his licence. "I'm not driving," he said. The policeman looked a bit bewildered, then came round to my side and asked what we were doing. I explained to him that we were driving from coast to coast to raise funds for Cancer Research. I gave him my International Drivers' Licence and my British one and he took them back to the police car to check up.

When he returned, he told us he'd been driving in the opposite direction when he spotted us going much slower than the rest of the traffic. He wanted to check whether we had lights and a triangle on the back of the vehicle. While following us, he'd noticed that the driver (which he'd thought was Mark, sitting on the left) spent a lot of the time looking behind him, which was hardly conducive to good driving.

Fortunately, he let us continue and even wished us luck. I think he was surprised that we'd already travelled so far. Fortunate, too, that the triangle had been displayed on the back – if only for a few hours...

With fifteen miles to go before Denton the trucks and cars were still whizzing past, but Nick had worked out an alternate route that ran parallel to the busy 380. The road was much rougher and narrower and meandered through the outer suburbs, but at least there were no big trucks thundering past at speed.

We arrived at our Super 8 Motel in Denton well ahead of schedule at 3.45pm. I'd arranged to meet an Aussie friend, Pete Pohlman, who just happened to live about ten miles out of town. Our fathers had been very good friends in Geelong when we were children and Pete and Debbie, his American wife, had invited us all to have an Aussie barbecue at their Texas home. But first Pete wanted to have a look at the Oldsmobile. Almost inevitably, he joined the long list of people amazed that we were driving such an unlikely vehicle for such a distance.

I was really looking forward to the barbecue – in fact, I couldn't wait. And it didn't disappoint. Nice, tender Texas steak that the knife cut through like butter and a healthy salad, washed down with a pleasant Californian wine.

100 miles.

DAY 18

Tuesday 30th April
Denton, Texas

It didn't take me long to realise that I didn't like days without driving. This would be our second scheduled day off the road and after all those days of sitting on the Oldsmobile and hearing that relentless, rhythmic chuff, chuff, I was once again missing it. How else could I spend a whole day? As the weather was nice and hot, well into the 80s Fahrenheit, and Denton's Super 8 Motel had a swimming pool near my room, I decided to start the day with an energetic swim to exercise the muscles.

Shaded areas are in short supply here so the chaps were checking the Oldsmobile while it was still in shadow. We then made use of the washing machine and dryer to get our clothes ready for the next stage of our trip.

But for no apparent reason I seemed to be afflicted with mid-term blues. That shouldn't have been the case. I hoped it wouldn't last. After all, here we were at well over half distance and hardly any problems had arisen with the Oldsmobile.

Pete, my Aussie friend, called in late afternoon after work to have a good look at the Olds, then the rest of the team went sight-seeing in Denton. When we drove into this University city the previous day it had given a good impression with well laid out streets, a population of over 100,000 and a very diverse economy.

Later, the rest of Pete's family met us at Outback, a nearby restaurant. It was appropriate for two Aussies to converge on an Australian themed place, albeit with a Texan slant. By co-incidence, our planned route for the following day went within a couple of miles of Pete's house. We arranged to meet so he could accompany me in the passenger seat for half an hour.

It had been a pleasant evening, in which my Aussie accent was once again revived.

0 miles

It might be green in this part of Texas, but it's also cold and wet!

I thought it was supposed to be warm in this country.

CPR weld the mudguard (fender) stay at Longview, Texas.

Crossing a river in Louisiana.

A trip down the drag strip near Port Allen, Louisiana.

On Bourbon Street, New Orleans.

Reluctantly, we leave Bourbon Street.

Near New Orleans with Mike and Dianne Seidermann.

New houses at Lake Pontchartrain following devastation by Hurricane Katrina.

Santa Rosa Island, Florida.

Aly's Beach, Florida.

Aboard the Batmobile at Tallahassee Automotive Museum.

With DeVoe Moore, founder of the Tallahassee Museum.

Mark and Joy study the menu at Goodman's BBQ Drive-Thru at Perry, Florida.

Picking up the order.

We made it! Ormond Garage on the Florida coast.

Maggie and John Lake presenting Joy with honoury membership of the Oldsmobile Club of Florida.

Daytona Beach at last!

The end of the road.

DAY 19

Wednesday 1st May
Denton to Mineola, Texas

After a not particularly appetising breakfast, Jim and I managed to leave more or less on time around 9.00am and moved out of Denton. This morning we were on the correct road; the driver had double checked the route the previous day! It was still a bit tricky though. We had to run beside the busy Interstate 35, then under a bridge at a hectic intersection which took us on to Highway 288. Heading north until we reached Highway 380, we would then turn right and head east into even heavier traffic.

We'd arranged to meet Pete at a Shell service station but when we pulled in he wasn't there. I wondered if we'd stopped at the right place, but I relaxed as he arrived a few minutes later.

It was fortuitous that we'd arranged that stop as a chap in a classic Jaguar pulled up and was more than pleased to meet us. He'd been following our progress via our website and was waiting up the road for us to pass him so he could take a photo, but he'd given up when we hadn't appeared at the expected time. We chatted for quite a few minutes until it was time to leave and Pete hopped on to the passenger seat.

I must admit that when I first sat on the Oldsmobile back in 2006 it had felt intimidating sitting so high up. With the road seemingly rushing towards us, the vibrating mudguards and lack of seat belts exaggerated the sense of speed. As far as Pete was concerned, I don't think the 380 was the ideal road for a first run in a veteran car. It was busy, and as usual the big trucks thundering past buffeted the car and its occupants. I looked at Pete and suspected he was trying to put on a brave face. After a while he must have become accustomed to his new experience, telling me that he was really enjoying himself. After about half an hour and fourteen miles from where we met up, it was time to make our farewells. One of our team had followed in Pete's car and after swapping places on the Olds with Jim, Pete set off back to Denton.

I was surprised how green the terrain had become with acres of corn crops and roadside verges bursting with varieties of grasses. We crossed over two lakes whose concrete bridges, similar to the one over Lake Bridgeport, were almost a mile long. After so many days of desert-like conditions back in Arizona and New Mexico, it was again a novelty to see so much water and felt almost like being on the coast.

We passed through the outskirts of McKinney. With a population of over 100,000, like most cities in this part of Texas it has a historical background connected to ranching, agriculture, cotton growing and textile manufacture.

Once on the 380 after McKinney I breathed a sigh of relief. The roads were noticeably quieter with an absence of enormous trucks. My passenger could relax and enjoy the scenery! This area of Texas gave a greater impression of affluence than had previous States but the next small town, Farmersville, demonstrated that life here was still not that easy, judging by the number of boarded up and abandoned houses. It made me wonder just what had happened to the occupants. We discovered that apart from its successful cattle industry, cotton, maize and onion growing activities, Farmersville's claim to fame was that it was also where the actor Audie Murphy grew up. I had to think hard who Audie Murphy was, then remembered as a youngster watching the occasional Western film with him in the starring role. During the Second World War he was the most decorated American soldier. Killed in an air crash at the age of 46, he was only this year posthumously awarded the Texas Legislative Medal of Honor.

62 miles after leaving Denton it was also time to leave the 380 and head south on Highway 69 at Greenville, another farming community. I spotted Mark and Nick at a service station and was looking forward to meeting up with them a few miles down the road, as it was close to refreshment time both for the Olds and for its driver and passenger. The service car and trailer swept past and about ten miles further on there they were, parked at the side of the road with kettle not quite boiling and something to eat, watched by several 'nodding donkeys' in a nearby field pumping up oil for all they were worth.

Highway 69 was much more enjoyable to drive along with very little traffic, a bright blue sky and the sun not too dazzling. The further south we travelled, the more trees we saw. I'm not a tree expert, but I'm sure they were a type of oak with small, bright green leaves indicating that spring had truly arrived.

The road wasn't entirely flat. Now and again we came to a rise but not one too taxing for the Oldsmobile as the speed didn't drop below 18 mph. The only time I used low gear was to take-off after a stop such as the occasional dreaded red traffic light.

Even more trees greeted the approach to our night stop at Mineola. Our motel was on the far side of town and while waiting at the lights about a mile from our destination, I noticed a man standing on the footpath pointing a camera at us. When we got closer I recognised Stuart Barnes from the UK. Stuart worked for an American Company and had driven down from Dallas to stay the night with us.

He joined us at the motel, which pleased Mark as they are fellow UK speed hillclimb competitors in the historic 500cc racing car class. After the usual Oldsmobile check-over (she came up fault-free) it was time to find somewhere to eat and for Mark and Stuart to catch up on the latest news – or should that be gossip?

Stuart had booked a place to eat back in town and we all headed off. At about 9.00pm we noticed speakers and equipment being carried in. Karaoke time, we were told. Time for me to move on, I thought. We hadn't quite finished our meal when the entertainment started. Amazingly, I was spellbound! Every participant was brilliant and all were singing Country and Western songs.

It became clear that this was the only place of entertainment in the town of 3,500 people. There wasn't one entertainer who sounded like an amateur – but then again they might all have been amateurs, despite their apparent professionalism. All the singers were white, but I did notice one African American helper who I smiled at when he was near me and asked him if he was going to sing. "Yes, later," replied Big Dave. I knew I had to wait for that. Wow, he was amazing! I thought I was listening to Louis Armstrong. If this is the kind of thing available in New Orleans, I can't wait to get there.

Back at the motel the temperature had dropped dramatically. By now it was night-time, so this was understandable.

115 miles.

DAY 20

Thursday 2nd May
Mineola to Shreveport, Louisiana

I got a bit of a shock when, early in the morning, I pulled back the curtains to check on the weather. All I could see were grey clouds and it looked as though it was raining. Not exactly what I needed to cure my mid-term blues. By the time I'd emerged though the front door of the motel the rain had stopped, but the wind still felt bitterly cold.

The first task was to go to the trailer and get out the small suitcase in which, several days earlier, I'd packed all the winter clothing thinking that from then on I'd only be needing short sleeves and summer stuff. Back at Denton, Aussie Pete had said that the weather forecast was not too favourable with an uncharacteristic cold front likely to put in an appearance. I chose to ignore the warning, thinking that in this part of Texas the sun would always be shining and it would be warm even when it rained. How wrong could I be?

It wasn't raining when Nick and I left, but the dark clouds looked threatening. We headed south on the 69 through oak forests and between grassy verges. The road was still damp and it was a bit frightening as the traffic was heavy, with big trucks spraying us as they belted past.

After about ten miles Nick reckoned we must be on the wrong road. The GPS seemed to be taking us to the nearest Interstate, which would explain the heavy traffic, so perhaps it had been set up incorrectly. Months back, when plotting the route, I'd listed all the towns we were to pass through on a daily basis, as well as the highway numbers, but in this case they must have been overlooked when the GPS was set up the previous evening.

We should have turned left out of the motel, travelled back into Mineola and then turned right onto Highway 80 which would take us in a south-easterly direction, rather than heading south on Highway 69. We'd already travelled ten miles, so rather than return the way we'd come we decided to turn left onto the old Dallas/Shreveport road, which would eventually intercept Highway 80.

The road was narrow with very little traffic as we wound our way through farmland and woodlands. This was much more pleasant driving than being battered about by traffic turbulence, but if only the temperature would rise! By now the support car had caught us up and we met at an intersection at one of the small farming towns.

After a couple of hours and about 35 miles we arrived at Highway 80, an older road without much traffic. Although single track, it was quite wide with adequate shoulders on each side and plenty of oak and pine trees lining the route.

The towns we passed through looked reasonably affluent with modern churches on both sides of the road. With all those trees about the area was not surprisingly noted for its timber and sawmills as well as for oil production and farming, with cotton the major crop.

All these towns had several sets of traffic lights and I was still finding the timing difficult, which as usual meant that rather than brake as hard as possible, I had no option but to run a number of red lights.

Descending a hill we heard a rattle and Nick found that a mudguard stay had broken. I stopped immediately and he made a temporary fix by tying it to the top of the trunk.

A few miles further on the support car was waiting at our service stop in Longview. Nick and Mark examined the mudguard and pronounced that we needed to find a workshop with welding equipment. Just across from where we were parked was a business unit, Collision Paint and Repair. Surely they'd have welding gear? They did, and as Mark is an ace welder he was sure they'd allow him to use it. The boss, who was a woman, was adamant that due to Health and Safety regulations none of us could even enter the workshop area. Two of her employees would weld the bracket.

Understandably frustrated that he couldn't be involved, Mark showed them what needed to be done. We were kept waiting for well over an hour, but the two chaps were very obliging and eventually Mark and Nick were able to refit the mudguard. We expected the bill to be quite high as the boss lady didn't appear to be at all interested in our trip, so we were astounded when she refused to take any payment.

Feeling confident about the weather, Nick had removed his waterproof overalls. The wind was still cold as we set off, still with about 70 miles to cover before Shreveport. We'd not gone many miles before the rain started, not heavily, but enough to get us wet and soak everything. My glasses seemed to retain the rain droplets and it was difficult to see properly. At least my jacket was keeping the rain off my clothes but as his normal overalls were now wet, Nick was hoping to see the support car before long.

The rain lasted for over half an hour and the wind still felt bitterly cold. I was not enjoying the drive today. Every hour seemed like three hours. At times like this I wondered why I'd elected to drive the whole route from start to finish. Today would have been a good day to sit in the warmth of the support car and let Mark do the driving.

I soon put that idea out of my mind. This trip was originally going to be an adventure for Trevor and me, back in 2009. He wasn't here anymore so I must do all the driving, for him.

Nick was glad to change back into his waterproofs at our next service stop, particularly as the rain started again just as we passed over the State line into Louisiana. What a welcome to the fifth state on our trip! I'd always imagined that the weather here would be hot and steamy!

Eventually we reached the outskirts of Shreveport, a city of over 200,000 people. Fortunately the hotel we were booked into was on the south-west side of town and although there were plenty of traffic lights, it didn't take too long to get there. I'd never been so pleased to end a day of driving and get into the warm.

Apart from the broken mudguard stay and in spite of the weather, the Olds had never missed a beat. Everything was still in fine order.

What a magnificent machine!

119 miles.

DAY 21

Friday 3rd May
Shreveport to Pineville, Louisiana

As Shreveport was such a busy urban area I was determined not to set off this morning on the wrong road. Last night I'd checked out the maps and memorised what I thought was the easiest route. Forget the GPS – it would just be a matter of going out of the hotel gate, turning left and continuing on the same road for several miles until we came to Highway 1. Then a right turn and we'd be travelling south, away from the busy streets.

Attired, yet again, in as many layers as possible to keep out the wintry winds, I was ready to leave at 9.00am. It felt extremely cold and dark clouds were gathering on the horizon. The rain, surely, was not far away and I really wasn't relishing the thought of driving through more of it. I remember saying that I'd never again complain about the weather conditions on the Brighton Run!

Just as Mark and I were about to drive off, the friendly hotel manager came out to tell us he'd just spoken to a local journalist, who was on her way to the Hotel to interview us. Twenty minutes later she arrived. I'd been sitting waiting on the Oldsmobile and felt bitterly cold; the wind felt as if was coming straight off the Arctic.

We finally left at 10.00am but at least the rain hadn't started. We drove straight along Hollywood Avenue. There was quite a lot of traffic (and of course countless traffic lights) but what surprised me was how rough the roads were. There were potholes galore and it was proving difficult to avoid them all. The GPS wasn't agreeing with the direction we were taking and was trying to get us to turn round and head for the centre of the city. Not if I could help it! If we were on the wrong road today it would be my fault and I was in no mood to change direction.

Highway 1 was easy to find and soon we were travelling on the dual carriageway through the out of town business area with very little traffic, but so many red lights that I couldn't help running a few. Fortunately there was no traffic crossing and no sheriff about.

After about 10 miles we'd left the built-up area behind. There was now an abundance of trees and large areas of swamp by the roadside. The highway was running by the Red River and in some low lying places, the water appeared to be flooding close to the road.

Many people in Texas had warned us that the Louisiana roads were in poor condition – they sure weren't exaggerating! There were so many pot-holes and so much water damage that it was becoming tiresome trying to avoid it all. The faithful Olds was taking it all in her stride, although after the previous day's incident I hoped the mudguard brackets would withstand the battering.

The clouds were still threatening at the first 20 mile service stop and although I felt a couple of drops of moisture, the rain held off. The insects seemed to like the low lying wetlands and bombarded us on our short stop. Whenever a train came near I waved, to check if the Louisiana train drivers were as friendly as the Texas ones. They were, and we acknowledged their whistle blowing.

After 50 miles we crossed a large bridge over the Red River, drove through the town of Coushatta on the way to join Highway 71. This was an area where the economy was once based on cotton cultivation which was dependent on the labour of enslaved African Americans. Since the civil war there has been much violence with various factions involved, but unfortunately we didn't have time to investigate.

Mark and I had stopped to check the oil level when a friendly Louisiana local stopped to ask us if we needed any help. We soon realised that he appeared to be on another planet – we couldn't understand a word of what he was trying to tell us. Perhaps he was on drugs, but we quickly went on our way.

As I turned a corner just exiting the town, Jim came running out to flag us down. The service car and trailer had pulled into the car park of a diner that specialised in hamburgers, so we parked up alongside. The owner came out to inspect our strange looking vehicle and told us in his quaint Louisiana accent, "Ah cook the best hamburgers in Louisiana." "Sounds good," I replied. My Australian accent probably seemed just as unusual to him as his seemed to me.

The idea of something hot to eat was too hard to resist as well as the opportunity of thawing out in warm surroundings. I was freezing cold and I also wanted a nice cup of coffee.

Whether or not the hamburger was the best I'd ever eaten I'm not sure, but it certainly was delicious and I soon started to warm up. The coffee, on the other hand, was not very good but the owner's hospitality was absolutely wonderful! I'd certainly like to return some day.

Time was marching on and we still had 80 miles to travel to Pineville. Once up on the Olds' seat I noticed the sun trying to break through and the temperature had risen a few degrees, so although it was still cold the driving became more bearable. Mark was keeping warm, though, with his impressive looking padded waterproof overalls and thick gloves.

We saw trees aplenty and the further south we went, pine trees became more abundant. We could smell the pleasant aroma of the pine forests – much more pleasant than that of the cattle and poultry farms we'd been used to.

It wasn't long before Mark heard a rattle. Looking behind he found another broken mudguard bracket. That would mean another welding job. With the amount of vibration and the rough roads that the Olds had endured over the previous three weeks, I was surprised that not more brackets had broken.

Nearing Pineville the road became busy. Nick was waiting to tell us that he'd found a back route to the motel that would avoid it. The road passed a dairy and other commercial enterprises, but it was in a terrible condition and I was pleased to arrive at the Sleep Inn. The time was 6.15pm. It had been a long day, but we'd arrived intact.

130 miles.

DAY 22

Saturday 4th May
Pineville to Port Allen, Louisiana

I had another surprise this morning when I looked out of the window. Clear blue sky and sunshine, a perfect day for veteran car motoring in Louisiana. The wind was still a bit chilly so I couldn't discard the wind-proof clothing, but blue skies sure can make a difference to one's mood! My mid-term blues were fading at last.

The previous afternoon, while looking for suitable places to film, David Winstanley had noticed large-scale road-works close to our motel. They were right on our route for today and appeared to be causing major traffic disruption for miles. There was no alternative route, so he decided to lead us as it might help us wend our way through.

The traffic and tail-backs started as soon as Jim and I set off at 9.40. I was concerned that if we had to sit in a jam-up for too long the Olds might start boiling. Although we could turn the engine off, only Mark and Nick knew the special technique for starting its single-cylinder engine and as I didn't know where they were in the traffic queue, to switch off would have been risky. Imagine sitting in the middle of the road unable to start the Olds and surrounded by impatient motorists honking their horns! We were lucky, the traffic started to flow before the Olds' warning whistle had a chance to blow like a boiling kettle.

We had to travel further into Alexandria before we reached Highway 71, which would take us south. The GPS was making its familiar noises to tell us we were on the wrong road and was trying to trick us into using the closer Interstate. My passenger did not seem at all pleased that I was ignoring the GPS and his instructions, but once we'd cleared the urban area about 45 minutes later the traffic seemed to disappear. It was much more pleasant on this smooth road surrounded by fresh greenery and small sugar cane plants, which stretched for miles and miles. They were probably planted not long ago and still in the early stages of development. The wetlands alongside the road seemed to attract a variety of fish and insect eating birds, among them herons and their small families paddling in the water.

Not for the first time I thought how lucky I was to be travelling at just 25 mph, allowing time to see the wildlife and observe its behaviour in a way that wouldn't be possible if we were whizzing past at 70 mph plus. As we drove through the small town of Bunkie the roads were much rougher. Bunkie had the now almost inevitable deserted buildings but somehow looked quaint however as usual there was no time to stop.

Thinking it was about time to have the Olds' oil level checked I realised that I hadn't seen Mark and Nick for some time, then on the outskirts of Bunkie I saw the support car and trailer parked in an abandoned service station, trailer lid up, the team relaxing in our comfortable fold-up chairs, mugs of tea in one hand, cigarettes in the other and with the kettle still boiling. Just in time!

I was keen to make our stop as short as possible but just as I was finishing my drink, a lady pulled up. She thought we were selling flowers from the trailer, then went on to tell Nick and Mark about her husband who was in jail for murdering her baby. I didn't hear all of it, but it made me even more anxious to keep rolling.

Every time I'd convinced myself that a reasonably smooth road would last for the day or the lack of traffic would go on forever, something would happen. Today was no exception. As I mentioned, the roads in Louisiana were not the best we'd seen during this trip, but suddenly the road deteriorated. It was as if a hurricane had hit it several years ago and it hadn't been maintained since. As the river, which looked at full capacity, was meandering alongside it I guessed the low lying roadway had been the victim of flooding as well as long-term neglect.

Despite slowing the Olds to 14 or 15 mph and sometimes slower, it was impossible to avoid the enormous pot-holes and ruts. After about five miles of bumping and banging the support car overtook us and we stopped, to give the Olds and its driver a rest from the dreadful battering. After being convinced that these road conditions would last for only a short distance, I started to fear that they might last all day. It was part of the main highway, so there seemed no logical reason why one part should be maintained and another neglected. We walloped and jolted along for at least another twelve miles. I started to feel guilty for the ordeal I was putting the Olds through and hoped that nothing would fall off her. If there was a Society for Cruelty to Horseless Carriages Over a Hundred Years Old, then I would definitely have been reported for brutality!

Suddenly, like a mirage in the distance, a wonderful newly surfaced, smooth, raised road appeared. On each side we could see much larger wetlands and a considerable number of birds, the majority of them herons. Presumably the improvements would eventually extend back to the road we'd just been over.

During our roadside lunch stop, David said he'd been waiting for us in Bunkie about an hour earlier as he'd found a classic car show and thought it would be good to visit. He'd tried to contact us by radio, but unfortunately the radios on the GPS systems had failed to communicate. He was disappointed and so was I. It would have been great to see a few Louisiana characters and some American classics at a Show, as well as to sample some of the local cuisine as David had been privileged to do. The participants at the show had all been told of our intended appearance and they'd been waiting with great anticipation for our arrival. I felt I should go back, but we still had some distance to go to our destination and time was not with us. Besides, I was not over-keen to make two more trips over that rough road.

About 20 miles from our Port Allen night halt, David was travelling just in front of me when we happened to pass a Drag Raceway. It looked like an event was in progress and he indicated to pull in to the entrance. I waved in agreement, crossed over the dual carriageway and entered the Raceway with the gate attendant looking at me as if I was bonkers. We could hear the roar of the cars going up the strip. David met the Clerk of the Course and told him about our trip, and the C-o-C invited the Oldsmobile to run up the track. I couldn't resist the offer.

While waiting for my turn I could see timed runs of around 4 seconds coming up on the clock, but at times it was hard to see through all the tyre smoke during the burn-outs. I felt sort of embarrassed. With a motorsport background in fast racing cars, I was now about to drive up a 1/4 mile drag-strip at a maximum speed of 25 mph, for which my time would probably be measured in minutes rather than seconds. I tried to make a joke of it, asking the startline official if it would be OK not to do any burn-outs. He was very obliging about our unusual car and told me to drive up the drag strip, turn around and then return in the opposite direction. Wow! We sure received quite a lot of applause and plenty of cheering.

I felt like spending more time wandering about the competition cars but had a nagging feeling that we should press on to Port Allen. Nick and Mark had already overtaken us before we'd entered the Raceway and I thought they'd be concerned that we'd not arrived at the motel.

We continued on the 190 until we reached Highway 1, which ran parallel to the mighty Mississippi. It was a bumpy dual carriageway that skirted massive oil refineries, then after five miles travel though the outskirts of Port Allen we arrived at the motel to find Mark and Nick, who'd been joined once again by Stuart from the UK. I guiltily apologised but they weren't at all worried about our lateness.

Stuart had driven for seven hours from Dallas just to spend the night with us. That certainly called for a celebration. After all our duties had been dealt with and the Olds put to bed in the trailer, we headed across the Mississippi into Baton Rouge, where we found a restaurant that specialised in local fish dishes.

118 miles.

DAY 23

Sunday 5th May
Port Allen to New Orleans, Louisiana

Before Stuart started his seven hour drive back to Dallas I invited him to accompany me to our first 'check the Olds' stop. It was 9.00am when we headed south down the quiet Highway 1. Quiet maybe, but this may have been due to the state of the road, with which I wasn't impressed. Perhaps resources are directed more to maintaining the heavily used nearby Interstate.

The sun was shining with the sky a magnificent blue, but the chilly wind still made it necessary to wear windproof clothing. Where was the hot weather that's supposed to characterise the south?

Highway 1 runs beside the 2,340 mile long Mississippi, yet we couldn't catch sight of the water. In an attempt to prevent flooding, a 25 foot high levee lines the banks of this mighty river, once the major transportation route to the north.

We entered Plaquemine, population approximately 7,000, whose magnificent 19th century architecture showed that its heritage was rooted in the era of sugar-cane plantations. Where once there were forests of huge cypress trees, providing material for a major timber industry, as with many European colonial settlements economic prosperity eventually took precedence over sustainability and supplies ran out during the 1930s.

Parked in one of Plaquemine's streets, Mark and Nick were waiting for us. While the obligatory photographs were being taken, the local Sheriff pulled up beside us. He was riding a quad bike on the footpath and seemed to think that what we were doing was crazy. After bidding farewell, Stuart set off in his hire car for the long trip back to Dallas while Nick and I continued along the bumpy Highway 1. Then, to my utter surprise and delight, the road became smooth. Perhaps inevitably, the volume of traffic increased when we joined Highway 70 just past Donaldsonville. On this trip, I never seemed to experience perfect road conditions for long. It was either smooth roads with heavy traffic, or light traffic but rough roads.

The time soon came to cross the mighty Mississippi. I could see the one and a half mile long Sunshine Bridge in the distance. It's a cantilever bridge with quite a high span so the approach road rises steeply. I tried to accelerate to a reasonable speed on the climb. Trucks were now overtaking us, but although the Olds' speed dropped quite a bit we were soon crossing the river.

I have to admit that being nearly 200 feet up and sitting open to the elements on the Olds, with the Mississippi below and being buffeted by the slipstream from the trucks and the occasional gust of wind, I felt a bit frightened. I could see the oil refineries on both sides and for miles across the flat flood plain, although I didn't spend too much time looking at the scenery. I was too busy concentrating on gripping the tiller and trying to point the Olds in the right direction.

I felt relief mixed with a sense of achievement when we'd finally descended to earth on the other side. With my Oldsmobile being of American manufacture, I wondered if she'd ever crossed the Mississippi in her earlier life. She certainly had now!

We now turned right on to a minor road, the 3125. This would eventually lead us to Highway 61, the road to New Orleans.

The countryside was flat and featureless, apart from small-holdings and fields of sugar-cane, and with the support car up ahead we decided to stop for an early lunch. I was expecting a phone-call from Dr Michael Seidermann, who lived near New Orleans and was the owner of a 1903 Curved Dash Oldsmobile. Michael had offered to garage our car for the two nights we were staying in New Orleans as he knew that parking would be difficult in Bourbon Street, where our hotel was. Bourbon Street was right in the middle of the old French

Quarter, where all the action is said to take place. Michael housed his own collection of cars in a small warehouse about 13 miles from the centre of New Orleans.

Ever since childhood I've had a strong desire to visit New Orleans and experience the traditional jazz clubs first-hand. I've always had a fascination for the piano and from the age of ten had piano lessons in classical music. My teacher was very strict and didn't know that when I practised at home I played traditional jazz. She would have been horrified.

Michael telephoned, saying he'd travel out to meet us on the 61 in a red Ford Thunderbird. We hadn't been long on the 61 when we spotted a red convertible Thunderbird with white-wall tyres coming towards us with two people frantically waving. Our travelling companions were soon behind us and a few miles further on the support car was parked ready for our fuelling stop. Perfect timing!

Michael and Diane were very friendly and offered to lead us to the garage via a more interesting route. We meandered along the River Road behind the Thunderbird, but because of the levee we couldn't see the river. We arrived at Michael's garage to find about ten assorted cars including, as well as his 1903 Olds, an E Type Jaguar and various Corvettes. My own Olds looked comfortable in her accommodation and we'd arranged to meet up with Michael the following morning, when he would take us to his friend's workshop to weld up her broken mudguard stay. As we headed into New Orleans to find our hotel and seek out the jazz clubs, I must admit I felt slightly guilty about abandoning her for the night.

The French Quarter was crowded. It was the last day of the annual jazz festival and many people, we were told, were staying on for a few extra days. It certainly looked like it, with people wandering up and down Bourbon Street in various states of sobriety – or in some cases a complete lack of it!

Several people had told me that I'd be disappointed with New Orleans as there's very little traditional jazz in the clubs these days. We wandered down Bourbon Street to soak up the atmosphere but the only sound blaring out of the doors appeared to be modern disco music.

Although the 'French Quarter' was founded, by the French, in 1718 most of the impressive buildings were built during the Spanish rule. The Spaniards had replaced the French architecture destroyed in two massive fires in the late 1700s and with their Creole influence, the buildings look unique. Bourbon Street's buildings are typically two storey with attractive wrought iron balconies, some more decorative than others.

In the early evening David, Eni and I met up to walk to Frenchman Street, where we'd been told we would find bars where trad jazz was played.

A band was performing on a street corner, attracting many onlookers who'd become absorbed in the tremendous atmosphere and were dancing in the street. It was impossible not to get caught up in the enthusiasm, until the police arrived and moved the performers on.

After visiting two more bars where a more modern style of jazz was proving popular, although not with me, I decided after all to have an early night. Far from arriving back at the hotel at dawn, as I'd envisaged, it was only 11.00pm.

As I was making my way down Bourbon Street one of the New Orleans Sheriffs called out to me.

"Why aren't you smiling?" Instantly I smiled.

"This is New Orleans, the place where you come to eat too much, drink too much, not sleep too much and always smile."

"This is the first time," I said, "that I've been told by a police officer to drink too much!"

He laughed and gallantly accompanied me back to the hotel. I was beginning to like New Orleans, but after sitting on a 1904 Oldsmobile all day for 23 days, I needed a little time to adjust.

95 miles.

DAY 24

Monday 6th May
New Orleans, Louisiana

At the start of out third 'free day' on the trip, Michael picked Mark and Nick up at the hotel first thing in the morning to drive them out to his garage, where they would not only prepare the Oldsmobile's mudguard stay for welding but spend some time looking over Michael's delectable cars.

I was due there at 11.00am to be interviewed by New Orleans journalist Reggie Fontenot. I arrived to find the rest of the team totally engrossed in Michael's collection. The interview lasted about half an hour, then we all went over to Michael's friend Mike Poupart's industrial unit for the welding ceremony.

It was clear from the moment we arrived that Mike was something of a petrolhead. Parked in front of the unit were several Corvettes and other American muscle cars in various states of completion. Inside there were even more, with a few being prepared for competition. Up until 2006 Mike's shops, Bowtie Automotive and MP Motorsports, were devoted entirely to Corvettes, their road and race car preparation, design, and build, but now he prepares other marques as well. Mike also drives in road racing and hillclimb events and has won both SCCA and four other national championships.

The motorsport involvement made us all feel immediately at home. Whatever the Health and Safety regulations may have been at that workshop in Longview, Mike seemed to be ignoring such petty inconveniences and while the mudguard stay was being welded, we all wandered about the workshop poking our noses into the cars.

Not wanting to prolong proceedings at the workshop too much, Michael reminded us that we were all due to go to his home, where Diane was preparing lunch. Time was marching on as a guided tour of New Orleans was on the agenda after lunch. Furthermore, he'd booked dinner that evening at his favourite New Orleans restaurant. What wonderful hospitality we were experiencing from people we'd known for barely 24 hours. And no matter how much we insisted, Mike at the workshop wouldn't hear of any payment for the welding job.

Diane had prepared a magnificent variety of New Orleans specialities and with the table laid out in the conservatory by the swimming pool, I couldn't think of a better way to spend time here. The speciality was poor-boys (or po-boys), a traditional sandwich on French bread. The variety we had was fried shrimp and roast beef, dressed with a salad. It was the best sandwich meal I've ever had.

After lunch we all went back to the workshop, where Nick and Mark refitted the Olds' mudguard. She was now looking ready for action again.

I tried not to remind myself that we were over two-thirds of the way to Daytona Beach, but in the back of mind I knew that we had less than 700 miles to travel in the next seven days. But being a realist (or should that be pessimist?), I was also well aware that the race is not over until you pass the chequered flag. I would have had sleepless nights if I'd analysed the situation more deeply – I was driving a 109-year-old vehicle with relatively fragile mechanicals that certainly hadn't been designed for such long mileages or tough conditions.

With time ticking on and everyone talking so much, Diane was becoming concerned that our tour of New Orleans would be too short to see much. We all piled into Michael's people-carrier and toured Uptown into the Garden District of New Orleans.

This area was once home to a number of sugar plantations until it was sold off in blocks, mainly to wealthy Americans who didn't want to live in the French Quarter with the Creoles. Originally it was developed with only a couple of houses per block, each surrounded by a large garden. In the late 19th century some of these large lots were subdivided as more people moved in. This produced a pattern for much of the neighbourhood, a block having a couple of early 19th century mansions surrounded by smaller, decorated, late Victorian houses. The grandeur of these dwellings made it easy to imagine the wealth and opulent lifestyle prevalent in 18th and 19th century New Orleans.

The tour had to be curtailed early, but we did at least get to see this magnificent part of the town. Michael had booked the table at BonTon Café for 6.30, so after a quick dash to the hotel to change we met Mike Poupart again together with his wife Patty, also a racer, who had won three national autocross championships. Tonight, we were going to be in esteemed company!

Michael has been frequenting the BonTon for many years and told me that he only ever has one dish – Crawfish Etouffee, a New Orleans speciality. I had to try it! It's a dish found in both Cajun and Creole cuisine, typically served with fresh crawfish over rice which was wonderful and unusually flavoured. If I lived in New Orleans I'd order it often myself.

After several hours of animated and interesting conversation I felt as if I'd known our new friends for years. We all had early mornings to think about and the team and I arrived back at the hotel at midnight.

Back at the hotel entrance, Mark mentioned that the night before they'd found a bar with real traditional jazz just up the road in Bourbon Street. It was late but I couldn't resist this – who knows, I might never get to New Orleans again. We all went along and, sure enough, the band was in full swing and there was room for us to sit.

It was well after 2.00am when we left. I had a very long drive in prospect the following day but it was worth it. I'd got to see and hear real traditional jazz at Bourbon Street, New Orleans – it can't get any better than that!

0 miles

DAY 25

Tuesday 7th May
New Orleans to Pascagoula, Mississippi

As we were in New Orleans, it would have been a missed opportunity if the Oldsmobile had not been filmed on Bourbon Street. We decided to meet Michael at just after 8.00am at his garage, then he'd lead the Oldsmobile for the tricky 13 mile trip into the French Quarter.

So after very little sleep we set off at 7.30am to pick up the Olds. Michael was waiting at his workshop ready to lead us back to Bourbon Street for the photo-shoot. In avoiding the Interstate we had a complicated route through traffic and back roads and I was pleased that Michael was leading.

As soon as we pulled up in front of the hotel the Olds was surrounded by tourists with cameras flashing. We answered questions for a while with, inevitably, most people not really believing that we were driving the Olds so far.

It was almost 11.00am before we left, Michael again offering to lead us out of New Orleans for about fifteen miles. Driving down Bourbon Street was a unique experience for me. The narrow street and historic buildings provided a good background for the film crew but I couldn't believe how rough the road surface was.

We joined Highway 90 that passed through some of New Orleans' outer suburbs. In Gentilly Terrace the houses were built on a ridge, making them higher than the road and guaranteeing that the area would not be flooded. Old oak trees lined the road and many of the houses were impressive two storey constructions. Here Michael pulled up and beckoned to us to stop. During Hurricane Katrina, he said, that this whole area was flooded to the level of the second storeys. It seemed unbelievable that right where we were parked, we would have been under 20 feet of water. The flooding had been caused by the nearby London Avenue Canal's floodwalls breaching in two places by Katrina's storm surge. Most homes required major gutting and repair work before they could be reoccupied.

Once through the urban area Michael and Diane stopped and we bid our fond farewells. I would miss them both, I said, as I felt I'd known them for a life-time and yet it was less than 48 hours. Michael told me that they both felt the same way.

Twenty-six miles from Bourbon Street the 90 travelled over the narrow strip of land, barely a half a mile wide, that separates Lake Pontchartrain from Lake Saint Catherine. On either side were new houses, perched on 20 foot high stilts, replacing the previous constructions that had been totally obliterated by hurricane Katrina. It was an unusual sight, some of the houses consisting of three storeys even on top of the pilings! I couldn't help wondering whether, if another hurricane were to strike, these houses would survive. After the devastation, insurance companies would not replace homes unless they were a certain height off the ground. Each area had different specifications unique to the tidal behaviour.

We continued along the 90 and over the mile-long bridge crossing the waterway connecting Lake Borgne to Lake Pontchartrain. In the days of sailing ships, this waterway was one of the main routes into New Orleans. The bridge was so badly damaged after Katrina's visit on 29th August 2005 that it was out of use for almost a year.

It was hard to realise that we were travelling through swampland. The road was raised and lined with trees which concealed the low lying water.

We crossed several waterways on steel bridges which were rusting quite badly. Twelve miles on we crossed the rusting Pearl River bridge and halfway across we arrived in the State of Mississippi, the sixth State on our travels. I'd enjoyed my time in Louisiana and felt a tinge of sadness at leaving it.

On the left was the small town of Pearlington, which was completely destroyed when Hurricane Katrina made landfall. We could still see the effects, with piles of rubble lying here and there amid the cypress trees. Every building and every vehicle had been destroyed when the storm surge travelled 4$^1/_2$ miles inland, drowning everything in a toxic mixture of water up to 20 feet deep.

The new two-mile long bridge at Bay St Louis looked impressive over the waterway, its dual carriageway rising in the middle to allow clearance for boats. I always feel slightly apprehensive driving across wide water spans, being wary of any sidewind likely to knock the Olds about, but she managed to pull well up the incline without losing too much speed and the gusts were manageable. When the previous bridge was destroyed the storm surge had been over 28 feet and many people lost their lives.

The 90 ran along the coast for about thirty miles, almost on the beach. The sand was a brilliant white but the sea looked rather grey. I'd been contacted by Carl and Marylynn Noacks, who wanted to wave to us as we passed by. If you're going to all that trouble, I said, we'll stop for a chat. We had to look out for a yellow El Camino on a pull-in at Pass Christian. None of us could see it and I kept driving, but a few miles further on I was waved down as Nick, while waiting for Mark and me to arrive for the refuelling stop, had noticed the yellow car and stopped it. We chatted for a while and our two new friends really appreciated seeing the Oldsmobile. Carl had lost his house and belongings during the hurricane and was just recovering from the ordeal.

It was now late afternoon and with over 40 miles still to go to our night stop in Pascagoula, we had to keep moving. At least the weather was warm and I was, at last, wearing short sleeves. After crossing more long waterway bridges we eventually found our motel just before 6.00pm.

It had been a long day but an extremely enjoyable one. We'd left New Orleans, arrived on the coast and seen the sea for the first time since we'd left California. And, best of all, the Oldsmobile was still running perfectly.

128 miles.

DAY 26

Wednesday 8th May
Pascagoula to Pensacola, Florida

It's so pleasant setting out in the Oldsmobile at the start of the day with the sun shining brightly and the sky a wonderful shade of blue. And I can't think of a better vehicle to be driving in such weather. Up on the Olds, I couldn't imagine sitting in a modern enclosed box, with the air-conditioning giving a false impression of what conditions are like outside.

When the weather's hot (which hasn't been often on this trip!), as soon as we start driving the Olds the breeze is enough to cool us down until we stop again. The answer is to keep driving!

The 90 headed north-east this morning and in just 30 miles we'd crossed another State line into Alabama, the seventh State on our trip. All roads, including the Interstate, had to skirt round the very wide Mobile Bay. This is a busy shipping area as the city of Mobile is the only port in Alabama.

The road was good and I guess fairly new, following Katrina's destructive visit. The grass seemed to be bright green and trees, mainly cypress, lined the roadside.

At the first service stop I noticed the atmosphere started to feel humid, which is what I'd been expecting, but didn't get, in Louisiana. Once underway again there was just enough breeze to make us feel comfortable. I was impressed by the efficiency of the Oldsmobile's air-conditioning!

Apart from a few small towns, the scenery didn't offer much variety until we arrived on the outskirts of Mobile. The traffic had increased and the usual traffic lights were presenting me with the same old difficulties. And yes, I did run several red lights. In fact I have to confess that this was the day I broke all records with a total of ten. I'm not proud of that but it was all done in perfect safety, although it was probably just as well there were no sheriffs about.

I wasn't relishing the thought of going through another tunnel. I would have done almost anything to avoid that but there was now no alternative. To cross over the Mobile/Tensaw River we had to negotiate the Bankhead Tunnel. As we were in downtown Mobile it was difficult to find a place beforehand to stop and turn on the red rear bicycle lights. Fortunately Mark was at the side of the road and I quickly pulled up while he turned them on.

This tunnel was scary – fairly narrow, descending steeply and running for nearly threequarters of a mile. Traffic was overtaking us rapidly and although it was well lit, I couldn't help wondering if other drivers would be able to notice our relatively slow moving vehicle in time. It was difficult to eradicate the negative thoughts flashing through my mind. I could see the end of the tunnel in the distance and the road beginning to rise before the exit. I hoped that at least the red flashing lights on the Olds would provide enough warning as we began to lose speed on the steep incline.

Then, as quickly as we were in one side we were out the other and I wondered why I'd felt so frightened. We'd made it! I'd looked at the map beforehand and knew that just out of the tunnel we had to turn right and head south. The intersection ahead spread out over several lanes and I kept in the right-hand one. My passenger, Jim, had different ideas and told me in no uncertain terms to get into the middle lane. "Are you sure?" I called out. There was no reply.

When driving an antique vehicle such as the Olds in heavy traffic the driver needs to know in advance the precise lane to get into. Unlike in a modern car, it's not a just a matter of changing down and accelerating away, you have to keep out of the way of traffic travelling at much higher speeds. This time I took things into my own hands. As the right hand lane veered south, immediately on my right between the lanes was a triangle of grass without curbing. I pulled the Olds onto this little haven, waited until the traffic had died down and then carried on to Highway 98.

The road then crossed a number of bays via long concrete bridges, one of them over three miles long. On some of them I was surprised to see people parked on the shoulder, fishing.

Passing USS Battleship Memorial Park, I could see the Alabama battleship moored and on display to the public, together with combat aircraft and tanks. The Alabama was active during the Second World War in the Atlantic and Pacific Oceans as well as having a temporary assignment with the British fleet.

With the 98 now following what was called the 'Old Spanish Trail', we saw many cotton, corn and soybean crops, with a mix of fruits and vegetables along the way.

About 30 miles after leaving the waterways near Mobile, the highway took us inland on a nice smooth surface through more small towns. The whole countryside was a lush green with many trees, again mainly cypress. After Seminole, a State sign told us we were now in Florida, the eighth and last State on our long journey. Our visit to Alabama had been a really short one, at just 65 miles. I suddenly became aware that we were nearing the end of this epic journey, but I had to start concentrating on the task at hand. We weren't there yet, at least not until I was looking at the Atlantic Ocean.

With about 20 miles to go to our destination at Pensacola the 90 split into two, one half going straight on and the other veering right. I chose the right-hand lane as I was sure that would be the right direction. Unfortunately, both the GPS and my passenger had different ideas. I ignored them both and carried on, experiencing no small degree of satisfaction when we eventually arrived at our destination.

When a journey like this is nearing its final stages, there are occasionally days when tensions can build up between driver and passenger/navigator. This was definitely one of those days!

On the outskirts of Pensacola I followed the signs directing us to the National Naval Aviation Museum, reputedly the world's largest such establishment. David had arranged a visit and had already gone ahead. We entered Naval Air Station Pensacola's large, 8,500 acre facility after showing passport and driving licence at a checkpoint. After a couple of miles of driving through well manicured lawns with a variety of shrubs and trees, we arrived at the Museum. It was massive, its car parks were over-flowing and there were crowds of tourists. I couldn't see David or Eni, so we phoned to find they were already walking around the exhibits.

I'd assumed that the Olds was going to be filmed amongst the exhibits but that wasn't the case at all. In fact there were so many people around that I didn't want to leave her in the public car park, so I elected to drive straight to the Days Inn motel, a decision prompted by the fact that it was on the other side of town and it was getting close to the 5.00pm rush hour.

After the usual urban driving hindrances like traffic lights, traffic build-up and a couple more wrong instructions, we eventually arrived at the motel to find the trailer, in which the Olds had been bedded every night, but no support car and no sign of Mark or Nick.

The motel receptionist told us they'd arrived earlier. Via our web-site they'd checked the Yellowbrick Tracker, which reads and transmits our location every hour, to find that we were at the Naval Aviation Museum. They'd decided to join us but hadn't realised we'd already left...

Eventually we all arrived back at the motel and Nick and Mark set about the usual end of day check-over. Mark noticed that the Olds' engine was running quite rich and on deceleration it had popped a few times, the equivalent of a human burp. It's easy to adjust the mixture on the carburettor and after several attempts and circuits of the car park, he was satisfied with the results.

It was soon time to find a suitable place to eat, which shouldn't have been difficult in this city of over 50,000 people. Because of its strategic position Pensacola had, at various times, been governed by the Spanish, French, British, United States and the Confederate States of America so we should, we thought, have a variety of restaurant choices. This wasn't the case. We ended up at an American style wine bar which served nice hamburgers.

110 miles.

DAY 27

Thursday 9th May
Pensacola to Panama City, Florida

Emerging from my room in the morning I heard a familiar chuff, chuff, chuff. I looked outside and there was Mark, driving the Olds round the car park with a stranger in the passenger seat. It was the manager of our Days Inn motel, who had kindly offered to give us one room free. He'd never seen a vehicle as old as this one, let alone had a ride in one, and he was most impressed.

After breakfast, Nick and I headed down the hill under a bright, sunlit and cloudless sky to the old centre of Pensacola, turned left for a mile or so, passing very plush two and three storey beachside houses, until we reached Pensacola Bay and turned right. Ahead was a long bridge that stretched into the distance for $3^1/_2$ miles. The bay was calm and an inviting blue colour, but with cars overtaking us at high speed I was pleased when we reached the end after some twenty minutes. After another mile and a half we crossed yet another long bridge then turned left on to the 399.

This turned out to be a wonderful surprise. The 399 went along Santa Rosa Island. Lying between Pensacola Beach and Navarre Beach, Santa Rosa is a barrier island of brilliant white sugar sand barely 2,000 feet wide with the road running along the middle of this natural sand dune. To the right, the Gulf of Mexico laps on the shoreline. Today it was smooth and an amazing azure colour. I couldn't have asked for a more scenic stretch of road along which to take the Oldsmobile. It was entirely undeveloped with no houses, condominiums or hotels in sight. I loved it!

I kept wishing that this natural unspoilt wilderness would last all day, but after twelve miles the 399 went over a bridge and we joined the 98 once again to continue east, more or less on the mainland.

I noticed a Model A Ford travelling in the opposite direction to us. The driver waved, turned round and was soon following us. When we pulled up at the support car he stopped for a chat. Mark had parked it in front of a small printing shop and the printer came out to talk to us too. He kindly gave us some of his printed bottle holders to take as souvenirs. The Model A driver had come out to see us from his home in Fort Walton Beach and decided to follow the Oldsmobile back again. I had intended to pull up later and exchange contact details but unfortunately he'd filtered off before I had the opportunity.

From Fort Walton Beach we continued on the 98 as planned but then decided to turn right onto the 30A, which ran along the beach-front almost until our destination at Panama City. It might have been a few miles longer but at least we could experience a seaside environment instead of running inland.

The scenery was in total contrast to the natural wilderness of earlier in the day. There were high rise hotels, condominiums, multi storey residences and even a few single storey houses. Judging by the level of traffic, it must be a popular area. Several major construction sites gave the impression that big money was being invested to replace the buildings destroyed by Hurricane Katrina. It was not until we'd travelled across the region for days that it became apparent just how vast an area had been affected by the hurricane.

The road then went inland, over more bridges spanning lakes and waterways. I can't remember ever crossing so many bridges in one day.

Further along Highway 30A we came to Alys Beach. After driving past two white butteries which act as the entrance, on both sides of the road were planted tall palm trees. Alys Beach is a purpose designed community with buildings, all in white, inspired by structures of Bermuda, Antigua and Guatemala.

I spotted David lurking behind one of the palm trees, film camera in hand. He called out to me to turn round, go back to the entrance and come through again, as all the modern cars behind me had ruined his first take. I duly stopped and returned, then waited until there was no traffic about and came in again.

With the filming completed, Mark had found a place for lunch called 'Georges At Alys Beach'. The tables were outside and I parked the Oldsmobile at the side of the restaurant where I could keep an eye on her. Rather than having a tarmac surface, the small side road was covered in sea-shells. It looked so unusual and blended in with the white colour of all the buildings. The surface was hard-packed and firm, the shells interspersed with brilliant white sand that looked like snow. This white sand is the result of quartz crystals washing down from the Appalachian Mountains centuries ago. With the crystals being continually ground smooth and polished, the surf of the Gulf of Mexico deposited billions of the grains as sand on the shoreline.

At Georges we learned that the development of the area is in its early stages and that if we were interested there were condominiums available for $6 million. We were forced to decline the offer!

Once we'd enjoyed the local seafood delicacies, with another 25 miles and more bridges to cross it was time to continue. I wanted to savour the Gulf coast for a bit longer as the next day we would start heading inland again, to the north of the State this time, until in four days' time we would reach the east coast of the USA and the Atlantic Ocean.

The dual carriageway was busy – with more traffic lights – and I started to long for the quiet and deserted area we'd just passed though. The Red Roof Inn was on the far side of town, which might prove to be an advantage the next morning, allowing me to head straight out onto the open road and avoid busy urban areas.

It was just before 5.00pm when we arrived at the Inn. Mark and Nick checked a creaking front wheel on the Oldsmobile and decided it needed another douche to expand the wood, which kept them busy for an hour or two. We then went and bought a takeaway up the road and all sat in the breakfast room of the motel, using it as our 'restaurant'. The service wasn't too good though – no waiters!

I was curious as to how this city of 35,000 people came to get its name. I'd been to Panama City in Central America when I was a child and while planning this trip years ago I was surprised to find a place in the US with the same name. I discovered that the original name of the town was Harrison. The name change took place during the building of the Panama Canal, as a way to link the area to an ongoing media interest in the hope of promoting real estate development in Florida.

110 Miles.

DAY 28

Friday 10th May
Panama City to Tallahassee, Florida

The decision was made to leave Panama City half an hour earlier than scheduled, at 8.30am. We'd been invited to visit the Tallahassee Motor Museum, which was 15 miles further on past the motel where we'd be spending the night. Just as we were about to leave, we learned that we'd be crossing the Eastern line later on this morning and the clocks would go forward an hour. In other words, in real terms we'd be leaving an hour later than we initially thought.

US Highway 231 is a wide dual carriageway that runs north of Panama City. I thought it would be easy driving with little traffic, but I got it wrong again. The road might be wide, but there seemed to be traffic lights every 100 yards or so, all geared to turn red just as I was approaching. I was proud of myself, though – this time I didn't run a single red light!

Surprisingly, after we left the million or so traffic lights and out-of-town shopping areas of Panama City, the road became much quieter. After 25 miles we turned right on to the single lane Highway 20. Where once there had been large forests, there were now just pockets of cypress trees here and there. During the mid 1800s cotton was the main crop in this area, the bales being shipped down the Apalachicola River then onwards to England, but all this ceased during the Civil War. By the start of the 20th century timber had became the main money-making industry. The large cypress trees, many of them over three hundred years old, were cut from the swamps then rafted and floated down the Apalachicola to the huge sawmills at the mouth of the river.

The roads were great as we drove mile after mile through the new young forests, then after Blountstown, we crossed over the River itself. I looked downstream from the bridge and imagined what it must have looked like a hundred years ago when paddle steamers, laden with cargo, cut their way through the murky waters on their way to the next port of call.

A mile further on we entered Bristol. It calls itself a city, yet has a population of only 800 or so. Its claim to fame is that during the fifties, a Baptist preacher proclaimed that this was the location of the biblical Garden of Eden. We didn't have time to investigate this, or indeed to travel on the Garden of Eden Trail. Surprisingly for such a small town I noticed three modern churches, coming to the conclusion that religion is popular here.

The smooth roads continued and I started to think I was going to have an easy day. I should have learned by now not to assume such things.

We arrived on the outskirts of Tallahassee and I'd never seen so many sets of traffic lights. They must have been waiting for me. As Tallahassee is quite hilly, many of them were on inclines and these, of course, were the ones changing to red when we arrived – hardly the right situation for the Olds to take off again. When the hill is steep it's difficult to pick up enough speed in low gear to be able to change into high. And that means walking pace!

Eventually we arrived at the Tallahassee Automotive Museum, twelve miles from the centre of the city. Opened in 1996, the museum was built to house and display DeVoe Moore's collection of fifteen cars. Because of its popularity it was tripled in size to 100,000 square feet in 2007. There are over 140 automobiles on display from an 1894 Duryea, one of the oldest automobiles manufactured in the United States, to a 2010 Camaro customized to look like a Pontiac TransAm. The 1860 horse-drawn funeral hearse reputed to have carried Abraham Lincoln is also on display. One of the most popular exhibits is the collection of Batmobiles --including the original cars used in the movies Batman Returns and Batman Forever, the Batmobile and Batcycle from the TV series, the Yellow Duck and the original Batboat used in the movie Batman Returns. I've never seen a Batman film so I wasn't that excited, but David insisted that I sit in one of the Batmobiles for photographs. I can now boast that I have sat in an authentic Batmobile!

We were all surprised at the eclectic mix of the other exhibits. These included what was reputedly the largest collection in the United States of case knives, outboard engines dating back to 1908 and Florida fishing lures. Other collections included adding machines, dating back to 1864, antique brass cash registers, electric fans, Native American artefacts, antique golf collections (clubs and balls), baseball card collections, motorbikes, pedal cars, and sports memorabilia. There were also smaller collections including baby bottles, baby rattles, beaded purses, can openers, pocket watches, telephones, typewriters, slot machines, and spark plugs – to name just a few!

I was even more surprised to find a collection of very ornate Steinway pianos, the one attracting me most being a reproduction of the 1913 White House 'Gold' Piano. It was so elaborate and ornate that it wouldn't be at all suitable for a normal house. I was tempted to get under the rope barrier and play it, but I didn't want to make a fool of myself.

As closing time approached we decided to leave, knowing that unless we did we'd soon be in the thick of commuter traffic. The Oldsmobile was parked outside the front door of the Museum and had attracted a few onlookers. As I sat up on the seat, museum owner DeVoe Moore came out to look and I took him for a short run round the grounds. I'm not sure whether he was impressed or not, but he found it difficult to believe that we had driven the car so far.

As I had driven more than my planned distance today, the Museum being an extra, I thought that it might be nice if Mark could drive the Oldsmobile to the motel, back the way we'd come. After 28 days of holding the tiller it felt frightening sitting on the other side of the Olds without anything to hold on to. Mark enjoyed his little jaunt and we arrived at the motel just before the sun set.

122 miles.

DAY 29

Saturday 11th May
Tallahassee to Cross City, Florida

Mark and I left the motel on Highway 20 almost on time. At least the weather was still warm – even humid – and I was wearing short sleeves. I was certain the winter woollies wouldn't be needed again. The tree-lined dual carriageway was smooth with very little traffic and for mile after mile there was little variation. After fifty miles of this we arrived at Perry, known as the Forestry Capital of the South because of its tree and lumber industry.

David waved us down on the outskirts as he wanted to film the Oldsmobile in a drive-through barbecue he'd found. The people at 'Goodman's Real Pit Barbecue of Perry, Florida' were charming and helpful, and we all had a few laughs when Mark and I drove through to order and collect our steak sandwiches. Not surprisingly, they'd never seen such an old car come into the 'drive-through' before.

Once we'd all scoffed our Floridian delicacies we needed to move on to cool off. The atmosphere was incredibly humid, but the breeze generated by driving along in the Olds was the ideal way to keep us comfortable. Once again, I was impressed by our vehicle's 'natural air-con' system.

During the morning the top of my back had begun to itch and the prickly feeling was becoming increasingly worse. Mark had a quick look and said it looked like a rash. From then on, each time we stopped everyone kept me at arms' length in case it was contagious. I felt like a leper.

As the day progressed so did the itching, I drove along trying to concentrate on something else, but came to the conclusion that I must have been attacked by bed-bugs the night before.

The scenery didn't provide us with much variety. After another 46 miles of green vegetation and trees we arrived at Cross City's Carriage Inn Motel. By this time the itching had spread to my front, my neck and my head. I was in agony and just wanted to scratch frantically, which would be the wrong thing to do. I looked in the mirror to discover that my whole torso was covered in spots. It could hardly be an attack from bed-bugs because it was spreading.

I tried a hot shower, then a cold shower but could get no relief. At the café next door we all went for a meal but I couldn't keep still and bade everyone goodnight. All I wanted to do was scratch to get relief.

I knew it would be difficult to sleep and it was. At about 2.00am I grabbed my laptop (fortunately there was Wi-Fi in the room) and searched the internet to see if there was something I could do to get relief. I looked under bed-bugs and found that there was an ingredient in toothpaste which, if rubbed on the affected area, may relieve itching. I was desperate and rubbed toothpaste over every part of my body that had a lump. I think it gave a little relief, but I never managed to get any sleep.

As I need to concentrate one hundred percent when driving the Oldsmobile, my anxiety levels inevitably increased when I couldn't drift off to slumberland. That night seemed to go on forever. I knew it would be hard to drive all day without sleep and we were so near to the end of this epic journey that I didn't want anything to go wrong.

By morning I was convinced that it was some sort of rash, but I never found out. I bought some cream at a Pharmacy and rubbed that all over, which did give slight relief.

96 miles.

DAY 30

Sunday 12th May
Cross City to Astor, Florida

Driving out of Cross City along the dual carriageway of the 19, with the breeze blowing through my hair and onto my body, the itching that had started the previous day decreased and became more bearable. I'd noticed a few spots on my face as well which, as I don't wear make-up, would be impossible to disguise for photographs. Oh well, forget vanity!

The trees and the vivid green, well-kept grass on the roadside and between the carriageways were similar to what we'd seen the previous day. I mentioned to Nick that although the landscape was very pleasant, I was glad that we'd experienced such a variety of scenery and terrain over the previous thirty days. If it had been like this for the whole trip I'd have become bored and the journey would have been far less challenging.

We drove alongside the Suwannee River before crossing it on the concrete bridge. This is a popular tourist area, its many natural springs providing opportunities for waterborne recreational activities. This was Sunday, and passing through the small towns we could see church car parks full to overflowing.

For one of our service stops we parked in the driveway of what looked like a deserted garage. It was overgrown with weeds and in front of the main building were seven abandoned and rusting American cars which looked as though they dated back to the fifties. It was a somewhat surreal sight. The cars would be ideal for a classic car restorer. As we finished our cuppas we heard a dog barking from inside the building. Maybe a retired person lived there and this was his classic car collection.

73 miles out of Cross City we entered the much larger city of Ocala. With a population of 57,000, Ocala is well known as the horse capital of the world. The equine industry is the biggest employer in the area. Employing over 44,000 people, it generates over $2.2 billion in annual revenue. The seven horsepower of my horseless carriage, however, was quite enough for me.

It was time for lunch and we found the support car parked at a barbecue on the outskirts of Ocala. It was too humid to eat outside, so we all went indoors to the air-conditioned diner. It's always difficult to find a small British-style sandwich in such places. I usually end up with more food than I can manage and today was no exception.

Just as I was getting ready to drive off, we were joined in the car park by another Oldsmobile. This was a much more modern, sixties version, complete with fins and considerably longer than my 1904 model. Pat and Kay Higgins of the Oldsmobile Club of Florida were on their way to a rally and had decided that they would intercept us along our route. They followed us for some miles and we stopped for another chat before they headed off elsewhere.

We joined the single lane Highway 40 and headed east through the Ocala National Forest. This was another area with natural springs and lakes that was very popular for recreational activities.

Astor Bridge Marina was the stop for our final night on the road. This single-storey hotel is built on the very edge of St John's River. 310 miles long, St John's is the longest river in Florida. Once busy with steamboat traffic, it's now largely reliant upon tourism and is a popular spot for winter visitors from the north and for fishing, hunting, and boating enthusiasts.

Nick and Mark checked the Olds for the final time, which meant that every nut and bolt was examined and every part cleaned, ready for the final day. Afterwards, we sat at a table on the pontoon that extended from the restaurant over part of the river. I was mesmerised by the bird-life and the ripples on the river, hoping to see an alligator swimming past. The breeze coming off the water felt so refreshing. Having hardly slept the previous night I retired early. It was just my luck that I missed seeing the alligator.

113 miles.

DAY 31

Monday 13th May
Astor to Daytona Beach, Florida

We'd been invited to finish our journey at the Birthplace of Speed Park, Ormond Beach, on the Atlantic Ocean nine miles north of Daytona Beach. Bearing in mind its century-old association with Ransom E Olds, the founder of the Olds Motor Works, this was an appropriate place to end our trip.

In the early twentieth century, most of the roads were unmade horse tracks unsuitable for the newly invented horseless carriages. Their manufacturers and drivers were continually looking for roads with hard surfaces on which they could drive fast and race each other.

At this time the Ormond Hotel was a popular holiday destination for the wealthy. A retired businessman noticed the hard-packed sand on Ormond Beach and thought it might be ideal for a race-track. The word soon got out and when a motoring journalist became involved, together with the managers of the Hotel the first time trials were organised on the sand in March 1903.

Two of the entrants were Alexander Winton in his Bullet and HT Thomas driving the RE Olds Pirate. Although the Bullet won, everyone agreed that the sands of Ormond Beach provided an ideal surface for racing. Thus the 23 mile length of beach was used for racing and land speed record attempts for the next 50 years.

To accommodate the drivers and mechanics, the Ormond Garage was built in 1904. Unfortunately, in 1976 it was burnt to the ground. In 2012 it was decided to build a scaled down version of Ormond Garage right on the coast, to house replicas of the Pirate and Bullet. The area was then named the Birthplace of Speed Park. I felt privileged to be invited to end our coast to coast journey at this historic venue.

It wasn't necessary to leave early on this last, relatively short leg and the final day of our journey. I'd already told one of the directors of the Historical Society that we would arrive at midday and from Astor to Ormond Beach was just 32 miles or a little over an hour's driving. Astor Bridge Marina didn't provide breakfast and we learnt that there would be no eating places until the outskirts of Ormond Beach, so Nick and Mark decided that when they'd found somewhere they'd flag me down.

I still wanted to leave as soon as possible after 9.00am. I was feeling anxious because I knew that although this was the last day, anything could still happen – we were close, but we weren't there yet! I wanted to relax and feel joyous on this important day, savouring every moment, though I was anything but relaxed and joyous as we were about to leave.

Jim was accompanying me on this last day of the journey and as we travelled through the forests of tall pine trees, I noticed two people standing in the distance near their parked car and brandishing a camera. I guessed they must have been there to photograph the Olds, so I decided to stop. John and Maggie Lake were from the Oldsmobile Club of Florida and intended to accompany us to the Birthplace of Speed. I mentioned that none of the team had had anything to eat yet, so they offered to lead us to a bakery that cooked what they said were wonderful breakfasts. They were right. We all felt satisfied after we'd eaten and for the first time the coffee tasted wonderful. No matter what we said, John wouldn't let us pay. Such friendly, generous people.

With just two miles to go I suggested to the rest of the team that they should get there first to witness the Oldsmobile's arrival. That short distance felt like the longest two miles I have ever travelled. There was heavy traffic and the inevitable traffic lights, sending my anxiety level sky high. Then suddenly, as I crested a small rise, ahead was the blue of the Atlantic Ocean.

I was overwhelmed; tears flooded my eyes. I looked up to the sky and said, under my breath, "Thank you Trevor, for everything. We made it."

A small crowd of people were standing at the entrance to the Park. I was directed to go over the footpath, through the entrance gate and park in front of the replica Ormond Garage.

Several Ormond Beach officials were there to greet us. Suzanne Heddy, director of the Ormond Beach Historical Society and Dan Smith, a member of the board of directors for the Motor Racing Heritage Association, expressed their gratitude for making Ormond Beach our official finish. I told them how grateful I was to be invited to end our trip at such a very appropriate and historic venue.

After a photo-shoot from our official photographers and the local press came a pleasant surprise. I was presented with honorary membership of the Oldsmobile Club of Florida.

We were invited to take the Oldsmobile onto the sands, a privilege I certainly wasn't expecting. I'd never experienced driving on such hard, compacted sand and drove the Olds down to the water's edge to signify the end of the journey. The temptation to carry on proved too great, so Mark and I took the Olds for several miles along the shore. We stopped, gazing out across the Atlantic to convince ourselves that we really had completed such an amazing journey. The trip was now over, but I didn't want it to finish. I just wanted to keep driving and so did Mark.

Back on dry land, we drove on to south Daytona Beach and the Atlantic Ocean Palm Inn. I still could not believe that my 1904 Curved Dash Oldsmobile had overcome such a monumental challenge with barely a hiccup.

She was, and is, an amazing 109-year-old horseless carriage.

44 Miles.

EPILOGUE

When the Atlantic Ocean first came into view at Ormond Beach, Florida, I have to admit that I was overwhelmed by the sight and with the realisation that after 31 days of high concentration, tension and determination we had actually achieved what we set out to do – drive a 109-year-old Oldsmobile from the Pacific Ocean to the Atlantic Ocean. I still can't believe it.

What really stands out in my mind is that amazing vehicle. Apart from a couple of hiccups it never missed one beat during the 2,903 mile journey. Considering the conditions it was put through it had every excuse. Over rough, pot-holed, corrugated roads; down steep mountain declines where I gulped at first sight, wondering if the brakes would be efficient enough (they were), up steep, mountainous climbs that seemed to go on forever; on many occasions the poor Olds kept up a steady 8 mph in low gear for almost an hour. What also surprised me was just how it pulled up those shallower mountain climbs in top gear. That was more than amazing!

Now, I know that back in 1904 RE Olds designed and built a brilliant car, but I have to say that the absolute reliability of this particular Curved Dash Oldsmobile was due to Trevor's brilliant engineering expertise, and the care and thought he put into the rebuild and preparation for the trip that he and I were originally scheduled to make in 2009. He had finished the rebuild just before he was diagnosed with cancer.

On that cold day in New Mexico, 8,000 feet above sea-level, when I crested a rise to view the most incredible panorama of mountains and mesas in the distance, I felt sad that Trevor was not there with me. He would have really enjoyed witnessing such a magnificent sight. Then when the Atlantic Ocean came into view my emotions again rose to the fore.

The journey could not have taken place without such an enthusiastic team to look after the vehicle. Mark and Nick maintained the Oldsmobile and looked after her every whim with such professionalism, every day and evening. For Jim's help, too, as part-sponsor, we are grateful.

I'd also like to mention one more person who had a great influence on my motoring life, my late father, Murray. He brought me up to appreciate mechanical devices and to treat each one with respect.

I hope I have pleased the two most important men that were so much a part of my life.

And there's my 92 year old mother who always encourages me to take part in these adventures while I still can.

Thank you everyone.